WF WRESTLEMANIA

The Official Insider's Story

Basil V. DeVito Jr.
with Joe Layden

ReganBooks
An Imprint of HarperCollins*Publishers*

WRESTLEMANIA: THE OFFICIAL INSIDER'S STORY. Copyright © 2001
by World Wrestling Federation Entertainment, Inc. All rights reserved.
Printed in Singapore. No part of this book may be used or reproduced
in any manner whatsoever without written permission except
in the case of brief quotations embodied in critical articles and reviews.
For information address HarperCollins Publishers Inc., 10 East 53rd Street,
New York, NY 10022.

HarperCollins books may be purchased for educational, business, or sales
promotional use. For information please write: Special Markets Department,
HarperCollins Publishers Inc., 10 East 53rd Street, New York, NY 10022.

FIRST EDITION

Designed by Joel Avirom and Jason Snyder
Design Assistant: Meghan Day Healey

Printed on acid-free paper

Library of Congress Cataloging-in-Publication Data has been applied for.

ISBN 0-06-039387-4

01 02 03 04 05 ❖/IMAGO 10 9 8 7 6 5 4 3 2 1

This book is dedicated to Tina,
who has been by my side through
all the losing and the winning,
and without whom I would not be
where I am today.

And to Alexander and Zachary,
who inspire Tina and me
each and every day.

I love you all.

Contents

WRESTLEMANIA IX
88
WRESTLEMANIA X
100
WRESTLEMANIA XI
112
WRESTLEMANIA XII
122

WRESTLEMANIA 13
136
WRESTLEMANIA XIV
150
WRESTLEMANIA XV
164
WRESTLEMANIA 2000
176

ACKNOWLEDGMENTS

The amazing success and growth of *WrestleMania* over the years is a result of the efforts of hundreds of people in the WWFE family. The passion and enthusiasm they bring to their jobs is unlike anything I have ever experienced anywhere else in the world of sports or business. I cannot possibly recognize them all, and I am honored to be a part of the group; however, there are many people who made this project possible, and I owe them special thanks.

Thank you to Jim Bell, for making this project happen. Jim has a unique combination of talent and experience and has been a great friend.

I would be remiss not to thank Toni Starson not only for her help on the details of this book, but for all of her efforts over the last fifteen years. Toni has seen every *WrestleMania* since 1986, and has been a big part of every one of those events. She might not be the best-known WWFE employee, but she is definitely one of the most well liked.

Thank you to Bob Collins, not only for his contributions to this book, but for his part in making *WrestleMania* and the *WrestleMania* Fan Festival better than we ever thought possible "way back when."

I want to thank all the WWFE family members who took the time and effort to share their memories and memorabilia with me. Liz DiFabio has been there since day one and taught me how to handle *WrestleMania* tickets when I was starting out. Liz found bits and pieces of history that I'm certain would have been lost if not for her efforts.

Thanks to Ed Cohen for his insights and stories. Ed is a guy who, in addition to knowing a lot about *WrestleMania*, also knows a lot about staying cool under pressure.

I am also grateful to all the people who helped amass the materials that made this project so special: Noelle Soper, Gale Tarzia, and Carolyn Colford for their efforts in making the pictures and images in this book look so good; and to Robert Mayo, Steve Cooney, Andrew Wilson, and those in TV production who made the DVD possible.

Thanks to Debbie Bonnanzio, SVP Creative Services WWFE, who is always ready to jump in and make almost any project happen, and happen better for her input.

A special thanks to Derek Phillips, who kept a creative and experienced eye on the progress of this book and kept us on track.

Thanks to Ed Kaufman and Scott Amann, who added their legal expertise to the creative process.

I am extremely grateful to Joe Layden, without whom this book would not have happened. Joe is a professional who taught me about the process and then walked me through it every step of the way.

Thanks as well to Judith Regan and everyone at ReganBooks for their understanding and support, especially our editor, Jeremie Ruby-Strauss.

I would also like to acknowledge some other important people. When I was young, I knew that when I grew up I wanted to be a man who could make a deal on a handshake and close it over a cup of coffee in a Styrofoam cup—a man like my dad. He ran his business that way, and regardless of the circumstance, a deal was a deal. I thought that this was an amazing way to conduct oneself, but I feared days of doing business in that manner were long gone.

Over the past fifteen years, I have had the opportunity to work with Vince and Linda McMahon in both the best and toughest of times. I have left their organization twice, only to return twice. I am proud to say that all of our dealings have been conducted on a handshake. And I've never had to question the validity of that contract. I want to thank them both for helping me attain that personal goal. More than anything, it has given me something money couldn't buy.

And, just so you know, Vince is a guy who can make a deal over a cup of coffee—in a Styrofoam cup.

In the spring of 1985, less than a month before the first edition of an event that would come to be known as the Super Bowl of professional wrestling, I had never heard the word "WrestleMania." I was living in Indianapolis at the time, working at a local television station. One of my responsibilities was to co-produce a weekly show starring Bob Knight, the volatile Indiana University basketball coach. This was the latest stop in a frenetic career that revolved around mainstream televised sports. I'd worked in and around the National Football League, the National Basketball Association, Major League Baseball, and thoroughbred horse racing. Since I have a somewhat unreasonable (and I suppose some would say unhealthy) fondness for stadiums, arenas, and racetracks, these were all jobs that suited me well. It had always sort of been my mantra, kind of a half-joking bit of bravado, that there wasn't a building in the country I couldn't get into.

My girlfriend (who has since become my wife) was then living in New York, and we were pursuing a long-distance courtship. One day, as I was bragging about my ability to get through the biggest doors in sports, she issued a challenge.

"Hah! You say you can get into any event, right?"

I laughed smugly. "That's right."

"Well, I want tickets to *WrestleMania*."

She was only kidding, of course. She was no more a wrestling fan than I was, but she thought it would be fun to watch me squirm a bit.

"What are you talking about? What's *Wrestle-Mania*?"

"It's an event at Madison Square Garden. Hulk Hogan is going to be there. So is Mr. T, and Liberace, and a bunch of other celebrities. And I want to go. You're such a hotshot—get me tickets to *WrestleMania*!"

I couldn't imagine what sort of circus would feature that trio in one ring, and I really wasn't interested in finding out; I suspected my girlfriend wasn't interested either. Nevertheless, I wanted to stick it in her ear. I figured I'd make a few calls, get a couple of tickets to *WrestleMania,* and by actually dragging her to it, be a hero and heel all at once. Boy, was I in for a rude awakening.

My first call was to Esther Rodriguez, a friend of mine who worked at Madison Square Garden.

"Esther, I need two tickets to this wrestling thing."

She paused, then laughed into the phone. "You're kidding, right? You can't get tickets to *WrestleMania*. It's sold out. Forget it."

"Yeah, yeah. Come on, Esther. Stop kidding around. I'll give you Indiana basketball tickets. Let's deal."

"I'm dead serious," she said. "These things are a hundred dollars apiece, and they're all gone. They've told everyone on staff here, 'Don't even ask.' It's an impossible ticket to get."

I was stunned. What in the name of God was happening to the world? I had vaguely heard of Hulk Hogan—I knew he was a professional wrestler and that he was popular. I had no idea that he was on the cusp of worldwide celebrity—that he would soon land on the cover of *Sports Illustrated*, and that the vehicle that would propel him to these lofty heights was something called *WrestleMania*.

I never did get the tickets, but I soon landed something even better.

An acquaintance named Jim Troy had been one of the World Wrestling Federation's first full-time employees. He handled their international distribution and is a guy with a big personality. One night, a few weeks after *WrestleMania,* I gave Jim a call and explained to him that I was trying to find work back on the East Coast. The very next day I got a call from Linda McMahon, the wife of Federation owner Vince McMahon, and a major player within the organization in her own right. Linda asked me to fly to New York for an interview, which I did. Within a week I had become the director of promotion for the World Wrestling Federation, and one of my primary responsibilities would be the marketing of *WrestleMania.*

More than a few friends and colleagues thought I had lost my mind, but I had done the requisite research, and what I had quickly discovered was this: the World Wrestling Federation was everywhere, and a lot of talented people were involved with the company. Dick Ebersol, who would go on to become one of the most powerful network executives in television, was working with Vince McMahon on a series of Saturday late-night specials. The catchphrase at the time was "the rock and wrestling connection," thanks in large part to the frequent presence of such performers as pop singer Cyndi Lauper.

Wrestling, by the spring of 1985, had become hip and cool. The World Wrestling Federation was on NBC, they were promoting live events at major venues all over the country, and they clearly knew what they were doing. I saw it as a great opportunity, a steppingstone to a higher level of sports and broadcasting. Little did I know that I wouldn't have to leave the company to get to that level. I couldn't have guessed that the World Wrestling Federation would become the cultural phenomenon it is today—and *WrestleMania* would become one of the single biggest events in the entertainment world. A ticket that was difficult to obtain in 1985 is now as hot as an Internet IPO. In fact, tickets to *WrestleMania XVI* were basically by invitation only.

I've been lucky. I've been backstage and ringside for the past fifteen years. I've been in the boardroom when story lines were discussed and celebrities invited. I feel privileged to have been a part of the remarkable growth of the World Wrestling Federation in general and *WrestleMania* in particular. I laugh now when I think back to 1985, and how little I understood about the event that would become a major part of my life.

The Super Bowl of professional wrestling? The World Series of professional wrestling? Maybe the Academy Awards of professional wrestling? I've discovered that *WrestleMania* is all of these things . . . and much more.

WWF WrestleMania

Main Event Tag Team Match:
Hulk Hogan (Champion) & Mr. T
(with Jimmy "Superfly" Snuka in their corner)
vs. Rowdy Roddy Piper & "Mr. Wonderful" Paul Orndorff
(with Cowboy Bob Orton in their corner)

**World Wrestling Federation
Women's Championship
Title Match:**
Leilani Kai (Champion—managed by The Fabulous Moolah)
vs. Wendi Richter (managed by Cyndi Lauper)

$15,000 Body Slam Match:
Andre the Giant vs. Big John Studd
(managed by Bobby "The Brain" Heenan)

**World Wrestling Federation
Tag Team Title Match:**
Barry Windham & Mike Rotundo
(Champions—managed by Lou Albano)
vs. The Iron Sheik & Nikolai Volkoff
(managed by Freddy Blassie)

**World Wrestling Federation
Intercontinental Title Match:**
Greg "The Hammer" Valentine (Champion)
vs. The Junk Yard Dog

David Sammartino vs. Brutus Beefcake

Ricky Steamboat vs. Matt Borne

S.D. Jones vs. King Kong Bundy

Tito Santana vs. The Executioner

Prior to *WrestleMania*, the World Wrestling Federation was really a nonstop fifty-two-week soap opera. Not that there was anything wrong with that—Vince McMahon has always known how to take the product directly to the fans and keep them interested and entertained. No less a marketing authority than NBA commissioner David Stern once said to me, "You guys"—meaning the World Wrestling Federation—"know how to market your product, especially in the smaller cities." But Vince was looking for a way to grow the business—Vince has *always* looked for ways to grow the business—and *Wrestle-Mania* would surely help in that regard. The World Wrestling Federation had always been an ambitious company. When a scenario or story line was particularly captivating or intriguing, there was increased interest, reflected in the live gate and the television ratings. Really, though, every week was next week. There was no beginning, middle, or end. There were peaks and valleys, blips on the radar screen caused by a visiting celebrity or a match involving a wrestler from another territory. But ultimately it was just a never-ending soap opera, a format that worked reasonably well, but which tested the patience of even the most loyal fans, and limited accessibility to new fans, who always felt they were on the outside looking in.

LEFT: The Hulkster and Mr. T grace the *WrestleMania* program cover.

OPPOSITE: Mr. T traps Paul "Mr. Wonderful" Orndorff in the airplane spin.

1

Madison Square Garden
New York City
March 31, 1985
Attendance: 19,121

The business was changing dramatically around this time. With Hulk Hogan as the star, Vince was putting in place a new vision of professional wrestling. He was trying to reposition it as "sports-entertainment." The majority of wrestlers in the early- to mid-1980s were not prepared for this transition. They were offended when someone said, "You're a sham. What you do is fake." But Vince wasn't offended. His response was, "What we do is entertainment, and it's the highest level of athleticism and entertainment you'll ever see. And what we do is damn hard. You just don't understand it. Think of it as a passion play. We have the athleticism of sport and the entertainment of a soap opera." In other words, if you'll just suspend disbelief, we'll deliver the goods.

Getting this message across was a challenge, mainly because World Wrestling Federation television at the time was a glorified infomercial, a way to entice fans to come out and see the product in person. The live event ruled. As a result, there was little in the way of shared experience. *WrestleMania* would address that issue through closed-circuit access. (Before the advent of Pay-Per-View, it was common for compelling athletic and entertainment events to be broadcast exclusively on big-screen televisions at arenas and concert halls throughout the country; if you wanted to see the event but didn't have a ticket, one of these closed-circuit venues was your only option.) It would be an event offering a common shared experience for fans of the World Wrestling Federation from coast to coast. At *WrestleMania* story lines would culminate and questions would be answered. In a sense, it really was the Super Bowl of sports-entertainment.

Of course, the Super Bowl wouldn't be the Super Bowl without a significant amount of hype in the mainstream media. This was another goal of *WrestleMania:* to provide a portal of entry—access to a far broader audience. How do you do that? By opening up *WrestleMania* to the press. This was no small step, for professional wrestling had long been a business shrouded in secrecy. But in the weeks leading up to *WrestleMania,* a decision was made: *We're going to have press conferences and we're going to issue press passes. We're got to give ringside access to photographers who don't work for the Federation. We're going to allow our talent to conduct interviews. We're going to throw the door wide open and let everybody in to sample our product. And once we've got you there, we're going to put Muhammad Ali in the ring, along with Cyndi Lauper, Billy Martin, and—oh, my God!— Liberace, and we're going to hook you all. Sports fans, boxing fans, rock 'n' roll fans, pop culture fans. Doesn't matter. By the time the press finishes reporting on this thing, everyone will be saying, "Man, I want to check this out."*

Rock 'n' Wrestling

The first *WrestleMania* was held March 31, 1985. The reason it was placed on that part of the calendar can be traced back to the early days of wrestling when there was a cyclical pattern to the business, especially in the Northeast. Typically, anytime people experienced a change in lifestyle patterns—for example, in the springtime, when days became longer and they could spend more time out-doors—business began to slip. The biggest falloff occurred after the shift from standard time to daylight savings time, which signaled a decline in business that would last several weeks, if not until the end of the school year. So *WrestleMania* was strategically placed at the peak of business—just prior to the inevitable decline. Today, thanks to *WrestleMania,* that's no longer an issue, of course, but the event remains where it is, much like a national holiday.

Interestingly enough, the date for *WrestleMania* was set before the event had even acquired a name. Vince knew that he could expand his business by staging a big, culminating event and broadcasting it throughout the country on closed-circuit television. Boxing in the 1970s and '80s had proved this to be an effective and profitable formula. You could have a great event in a great building (like Madison Square Garden) and sell tickets at a premium price, but if you wanted to make additional money, closed-circuit was the way to go.

Already in Vince's mind was the notion that the way to expand the audience of the World Wrestling Federation was through a connection to younger fans, and the way to do that was to infuse the live event with a higher degree of entertainment in terms of music, costumes, and dramatic entrances. Vince looked at MTV, which was still in its infancy, and saw the future of his business. And so there was crossover between the two worlds: pop stars featured in wrestling events, and wrestling specials on MTV.

Girls Just Want to Have Fun

The most enthusiastic and convincing rock performer featured in the Federation was, of course, Cyndi Lauper, whose involvement stemmed largely from the fact that her manager, David Wolfe, was a big wrestling fan. They thought it might be a good promotional opportunity for Cyndi, and so

they began to think of ways in which she could be woven into the story line. Eventually Cyndi developed an electric love-hate relationship with Captain Lou Albano, a fast-talking wrestler-turned-manager who had become one of the mainstays of the company. Captain Lou appeared in the video of Cyndi's "Girls Just Want to Have Fun," and Cyndi herself became the manager of Wendi Richter. What might have been just a lark actually developed into one of the World Wrestling Federation's most popular and compelling story lines, so much so that Cyndi and Captain Lou were among the biggest draws at an event just six weeks before *WrestleMania* itself. The event, known as "The War to Settle the Score," was originally intended to be the culmination of the "Rock 'n' Wrestling Connection," but it turned out to be much more. Rather than marking the end of anything, it signaled the beginning of an intense buildup to what would become the most important event in sports-entertainment.

"The War to Settle the Score," broadcast in February 1985 live on MTV, did not settle the score. In fact, what it did was create all this conflict that would have to be resolved six weeks later at Madison Square Garden, in the big closed-circuit event. One of MTV's producers at the time was Joe Davola. Joe was a long-time wrestling fan who had worked on a couple of shows with the World Wrestling Federation, so he understood the way sports-entertainment worked. Yet he remembers feeling an overwhelming sense of anxiety as that night dragged on, apparently with no hope of hitting the main event on schedule.

"At nine-thirty there were still two preliminary matches to go," Joe recalls. "And I was absolutely panicked. I couldn't believe they were going to be late. I had told everyone that we had to be ready to go at exactly ten o'clock with the main event match. For the last thirty minutes I was sweating bullets. All I remember them telling me in the back was, 'Just relax. Everything will be fine.' And I left there that night with a

TOP: Richter and Lauper exult in the center of the ring.

LEFT: The singing siren and her grappling protégée.

new understanding of how wrestling worked. Because, some-how, those two matches went off perfectly—bang-bang. And right at ten o'clock we hit the music and the main event began, and everyone in the building went crazy. It was a great television event."

Liberace and the Rockettes do the can-can.

It was also the perfect tease to *WrestleMania*. Credit for the name, incidentally, is generally given to Howard Finkel, known to many fans as one of the World Wrestling Federation's announcers. Howard is the unofficial company historian and fact-finder, and the nuggets he unearths are affectionately known as "Finkel Facts." For example, Vince might say in a meeting, "Howard, when was the last steel cage match in Pitts-burgh?" And Howard will say, "Ahh . . . December . . . 1981." That's a Finkel Fact. It's sort of a Finkel Fact *about* Finkel that in a legendary meeting in the winter of 1985, while a roomful of staffers were trying to think of a name for their big closed-circuit event, Howard Finkel blurted out, "There's *Beatlemania,* right? Why not *WrestleMania*?" And that was that. *WrestleMania* was born.

There was never any doubt as to where the first edition of *WrestleMania* would be held. Vince's grandfather, Jess McMahon, was the first wrestling promoter for the original Madison Square Garden, which was built in the 1920s. Jess McMahon is widely credited with transforming professional wrestling from a vaudevillian sideshow to a sports attrac-tion. The McMahon family has played Madison Square Garden consistently for the past eighty years, and Vince's father is in the Madison Square Garden Hall of Fame. Vince is known to quote his father by saying, "The Garden is the Garden is the Garden." In other words, it's the Mecca of our business. So there was no other venue considered. *Wrestle Mania* would be held at Madison Square Garden. The top ticket price would be one hundred dollars, which at the time was an unheard-of amount of money to charge for a wrestling event. Or so it seemed.

A Star-Studded Lineup The card at *WrestleMania* included most of the top stars of that era: Hulk Hogan, Andre the Giant, Big John Studd, Rowdy Roddy Piper, Paul Orndorff. Yet it's fair to say that if ever a major wrestling event was less about wrestling than celebrity, *WrestleMania* was it. The main event was a tag team match fea-turing Hogan, the Federation champion, and Mr. T against Piper and Orndorff. The teaming of Hogan and Mr. T might seem strange in retrospect, but it made perfect sense at the time. Mr. T was a former bouncer and toughman contest champion who had been reborn as

an actor. Both he and Hogan, in fact, had squared off against Sylvester Stallone in the third chapter of the *Rocky* saga—Hogan as a frightening and overzealous wrestler named Thunderlips and Mr. T as the snarling and heavy-fisted Clubber Lang. Mr. T had also gone on to star in the popular television series *The A-Team*.

But that was only the beginning. Thanks in no small part to the efforts of a man named Ed Cohen, who was one of the first employees hired by Vince McMahon, *Wrestle-Mania* also featured an eclectic—some would say bizarre—array of stars from the entertainment and sports worlds. Liberace, the elegant and outrageous Las Vegas pianist, served as timekeeper for the main event (after high-stepping into the ring with the Radio City Music Hall Rockettes). Billy Martin, the hotheaded manager of the New York Yankees, was the ring announcer. And Muhammad Ali, The Greatest of All Time, was the guest referee.

Of these, Mr. T proved to be the biggest handful. He was very taken with his own stardom, which wouldn't have been such a big deal if he hadn't also been more "show" than "go." He was not nearly the athlete that the World Wrestling Federation stars were, and he didn't work out like them. He had neither the strength nor the ambition to train with these guys. After a long day of traveling, meeting with the press, or whatever, guys like Hulk Hogan and Randy Savage would always hit the weight room. They understood that maintaining a certain level of physical conditioning was vital to being able to take the beatings demanded by their job. And to just keep looking good. So they would invite Mr. T to work out with them, but he almost always found a way to beg off. I think he worked out with them once and saw they were in a different league.

Opposites attract: Liberace and Billy Martin.

ABOVE: Hogan pumps up Mr. T.

RIGHT: The TV star urges the Hulkster to hit the heavy bag.

Eventually, the pressure got to Mr. T. In the tense and exhausting weeks leading up to *WrestleMania,* when he and Hulk were traveling around the country, conducting interviews and posing for photographers, Ed Cohen got a call from a co-worker.

"We've got a problem," the caller said.

"What's that?" Ed replied.

"Mr. T just fired one of our employees!" The guy didn't do something that Mr. T wanted him to do, and T said, "Hey, man, you're fired!"

Ed just laughed. "Keep the guy away from T. Let him think he's really fired."

That's the way it worked—anything to keep talent happy. In truth, much of the preparation for *WrestleMania* was done on a wing and a prayer. The World Wrestling

Federation had perhaps twenty full-time employees, and none of them had ever seen anything like what they were experiencing. It was inevitable that there would be problems both big and small. For example, Ed Cohen received another call less than twenty-four hours before *WrestleMania*—this one from Vince McMahon himself.

"Ed," he said. "I have a feeling that Ali is not going to show up with a referee's uniform. So you've got to get out to a sporting goods store and buy one. Shoes, shirt, the works."

Ed didn't flinch. "What size does he wear?"

"I don't know. Take your best guess."

And so, we know that Muhammad Ali wears size eleven and a half shoes . . . or at least he did on March 31, 1985, because that's what Ed bought, and that's what Ali wore.

Somehow, though, *WrestleMania* went off without a hitch. Madison Square Garden was sold out well in advance, and nearly one million fans paid to see the event at closed-circuit outlets across the country. They watched Wendi Richter recapture the Women's Championship with Cyndi Lauper in her corner. They watched Andre the Giant win a fifteen-thousand-dollar body slam match against Big John Studd. And finally, they watched Hulk Hogan cover Paul Orndorff—*one-two-three!*—in the center of the ring, in the tag team main event.

In a sense, though, the spirit of *WrestleMania*—the thing that made it truly unique—can be found in a story told by Linda McMahon. Less than an hour before the start of the event, as Linda was standing just inside the rear entrance to Madison Square Garden, she was approached by a group of Hell's Angels. Somehow, they had gotten in the loading dock and past the final security checkpoint. "So now it was just little old me standing between these bikers and the backstage area," Linda recalls. "They were bound and determined that they were going to be at *WrestleMania*. That the event was sold out and they were in a restricted area couldn't have mattered less."

So what did she do?

"We got 'em chairs," Linda says with a laugh.

That's *WrestleMania*. The idea that a group of Hell's Angels would want to go to an event that featured Liberace and the Rockettes sort of puts the whole thing in perspective. *WrestleMania* was an invitation to people from all walks of life. It was a way of saying, "Hey, America, the door is open. You might want to check us out."

ABOVE: Ali, Liberace, and the Hulkster meet the press.

OPPOSITE: Andre bashes Studd in their body slam challenge.

OPPOSITE INSET: Andre relaxes with a young Stephanie McMahon.

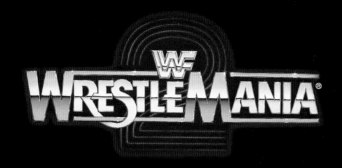

World Wrestling Federation Title Match:

Hulk Hogan (Champion)

vs. King Kong Bundy (managed by Bobby "The Brain" Heenan)

Open Invitational Twenty-Man Over-the-Top-Rope Battle Royal:

National Football League Players square off against
the Best of the World Wrestling Federation Superstars
(with special guest referees Dick Butkus and Ed "Too Tall" Jones)

Special Boxing Match:

Rowdy Roddy Piper (with Lou Duva in his corner)

vs. Mr. T (with Joe Frazier in his corner)

World Wrestling Federation Intercontinental Title Match:

Randy "Macho Man" Savage (Champion)

vs. George "The Animal" Steele

World Wrestling Federation Tag Team Title Match:

Greg "The Hammer" Valentine & Brutus Beefcake (Champions)

vs. The British Bulldogs (managed by Captain Lou Albano)

World Wrestling Federation Women's Championship Title Match:

The Fabulous Moolah vs. Velvet McIntyre

"Mr. Wonderful" Paul Orndorff vs. The Magnificent Muraco

Jake "The Snake" Roberts vs. George Wells

Corporal Kirchner vs. Nikolai Volkoff

Ricky "The Dragon" Steamboat vs. Hercules Hernandez

Uncle Elmer vs. Adorable Adrian Adonis

Tito Santana & The Junk Yard Dog vs. Terry & Hoss Funk

In the wake of the success of

WrestleMania, it was obvious that this would not be a one-time event. But as 1985 gave way to 1986 and planning for *WrestleMania 2* began in earnest, one question loomed above all others: *How can we make it even better?* Vince McMahon had a truly unique idea for accomplishing this goal. He wanted to divide *WrestleMania 2* into three separate events—each as big and bold as the inaugural *Wrestle-Mania.* The plan was to stage *WrestleMania 2* in three different time zones, in three different buildings.

By this time I was director of marketing, and to be honest, when Vince first suggested this approach, I had serious doubts that it would succeed. In fact, I was more than a little shaken. Three sites in three cities tripled the work. We'd need three times as many celebrities, three times as many wrestlers, three times as much money . . . three times the luck. But Vince was not a small thinker, and is not the type of man to be discouraged by seemingly impossible tasks. He wanted *WrestleMania 2* to be bigger than *WrestleMania,* and whatever else this plan may have been, it was undeniably *bigger.*

We eventually settled on the Nassau Coliseum on Long Island, the Rosemont Horizon in Chicago, and the Sports Arena in Los Angeles. We'd move from east to west, with an hour-long event in New York, followed by an hour-long event in Chicago, and finally an hour-long event in LA. Fans in each building, of course, would be able to watch action from the other sites on large-screen televisions.

OPPOSITE: King Kong Bundy Irish whips Hogan across the ring in their cage match.

(Since these devices were not yet standard equipment on arena scoreboards, they'd have to be installed and lowered from the roof.) Additionally, we planned to broadcast the event at more than two hundred closed-circuit venues throughout the country. In short, it was a mammoth undertaking, the complexity of which was compounded when we decided to move the event from its original date during the final weekend of March to April 7, so that it wouldn't conflict with the NCAA basketball tournament. That proved to be something of a nightmare, but eventually it all came together and the date and sites were finalized.

Hyping the Event

In preparing for *WrestleMania 2* we tried to re-create some of the better aspects of the *WrestleMania* promotion: appearances on MTV, press conferences, television interviews. We even brought Mr. T back into the fold, this time as a competitor in a boxing match against Roddy Piper. What we didn't realize, at first, was that because this match would take place in the New York venue, we were bound by the rules of the New York State Athletic Commission. That the match was clearly just an exhibition, and not an actual athletic event, did not matter. The commission insisted on an official weigh-in and physicals, and that we follow all the proper procedures for a competitive boxing match.

So, about two weeks prior to *WrestleMania 2*, I flew in a small chartered plane with Mr. T and Roddy Piper to Albany, New York, where a midlevel boxing card was scheduled. We then drove to a Holiday Inn, where a cattle call of a weigh-in was being held for the next day's fight. The only way we had gotten Mr. T to agree to any of this was by telling him there would be several important members of the media at the weigh-in, and that it would be a good opportunity to hype the event, as well as his own career.

We checked into the hotel about an hour before the weigh-in. Mr. T and Roddy went to their respective rooms, and I headed for the ballroom where the weigh-in was to be conducted. As I entered the room, my heart sank. Our presence at the weigh-in was a last-minute decision, and obviously word had not leaked out, since the single media representative in the room was a lonely-looking man from a local cable access channel (this, incidentally, despite the fact that the card included a promising young heavyweight from nearby Catskill named Mike Tyson).

I quickly tracked down Roddy and explained the situation.

"It's bad," I said. "There's one little camera out there. I can't even try to put a good spin on it. But this is something we just have to do. It's a function we have to get through. Once we get Mr. T into the room, everything will be okay."

Roddy was a pro. He nodded. "All right. I know what to do."

He marched down the hall and banged on Mr. T's door. "Come on, T! This is it! Let's go! They're waiting!"

Roddy screamed and ranted until Mr. T opened the door. Then they walked down the hallway together until they reached the entrance to the ballroom.

"Put your game face on, man," Roddy said. He was doing his best to get Mr. T all jazzed up. "Go in there, give 'em hell, and I'll come in later and do my thing."

With that, Roddy shoved Mr. T through the door. I hooked him by the arm, coaxed him to the scale, and got through the actual weigh-in as quickly as possible. Then Roddy burst into the room, a complete live wire, so animated you would have thought every network and newspaper in the country was there. He howled and spat and taunted Mr. T. In a near-empty room, he put on an incredible show. And we got through it. On the way home Mr. T kept saying, "How important could it have been? There was no one there." Roddy would just smile. That's typical of how some of the guys in this business—the good guys—operate. They understand what the business is all about. And Roddy was definitely a good guy. I asked favors like this from time to time, usually on the road, and I don't remember him ever saying no. Hulk Hogan, for the most part, was the same way. Randy Savage, too. These were men who knew their roles and understood their responsibilities. They "got it," which is an enormously important trait for any celebrity.

New York   The match between Mr. T and Roddy Piper headlined the New York event. Both men had some significant experience as boxers—Mr. T in his role as Clubber Lang and as a "toughman" competitor, and Roddy as a former Golden Gloves participant. Former heavyweight champ Joe Frazier worked Mr. T's corner. In fact, during the six-week promotional period, we even took T down to Smokin' Joe's gym in Philly and did a whole "Rocky" thing—videos of Joe working out with Mr. T, telling him what do, Mr. T running and training and throwing jabs in the air. Mr. T had a pretty big ego and could be both good and bad on the road, but he worked hard at the promotion of *WrestleMania 2*, and it paid off.

The New York portion of *WrestleMania 2* began with Ray Charles singing a brilliant, soulful rendition of "America the Beautiful." Joan Rivers was the ring announcer, and Susan St. James (who happened to be the wife of Dick Ebersol) was the guest commentator. And that was merely the beginning. The judges were G. Gordon Liddy, jazz musician Cab Calloway, and NBA star Darryl Dawkins. Lou Duva, a veteran trainer and a fixture in the boxing world, worked Roddy Piper's corner to balance the presence of Joe Frazier.

As for the match itself, well, it's kind of like the old joke: *There was a fight, and a hockey game broke out.* In this case, there was a boxing match and a wrestling match broke out. The trick in dealing with celebrities at *Wrestle-*

The stars come out at *WrestleMania 2*: Joan Rivers; Cab Calloway with Smokin' Joe Frazier; Ray Charles; Susan St. James.

Mania is to get the most out of their star power without hurting or embarrassing them in any way. So we wanted Mr. T to look good. At the same time, Roddy Piper was one of our mainstays, someone we needed every day. We had to find a way to make the fans feel they got their money's worth, and yet not hurt the reputation of the celebrity (Mr. T) or the positioning of the talent (Roddy Piper). Roddy, as the legitimate tough guy on the World Wrestling Federation roster, had to be able to do well. But, of course, Mr. T didn't want to come in just to get knocked out. That's part of what makes it so intriguing to incorporate celebrities into the action. Everyone knows the outcome is predetermined and that professional wrestling is entertainment, not pure competition. Still . . . the event is just a little bit more exciting, and there's a little more tension, when the celebrity is slightly unsure. After all, he's standing in a ring in front of 18,000 people. He's wearing boxing gloves, and so is the man in front of him. And these wrestlers are always wide-eyed and loud and . . . well, you just never know.

What happened in the end was that both men engaged in a bit of legitimate boxing. Roddy slipped in a few decent punches, just to make it clear that he was in control, but nothing that would have caused Mr. T any lasting damage. As the match neared its conclusion, Roddy executed a body slam on Mr. T, effectively ending the match. Since this was supposed to be a boxing match, however, Roddy was immediately disqualified. Mr. T was declared the winner, both men walked away with their reputations intact, and the crowd at the Nassau Coliseum roared its approval.

Chicago   The Rosemont Horizon was the site of the most unique match in *WrestleMania 2*—a twenty-man, over-the-top-rope battle royal, in which the last man standing in the ring would be declared the winner. Since this was 1986 and the Chicago Bears had just won the Super Bowl, a football theme was in order. The guest referees would be Bears Hall-of-Famer Dick Butkus and former Dallas Cowboys superstar Ed "Too Tall" Jones. Heavy metal singer Ozzy Osbourne, who was at the peak of his bizarre, unpredictable, bat-biting fame, would make a guest appearance, just for shock value. And the ring would be filled with not only such World Wrestling Federation stalwarts as Andre the Giant, Bruno Sammartino, Big John Studd, and Pedro Morales, but also an all-pro lineup of current and former National

TOP: Frazier cheers on Mr. T from his corner.

ABOVE: G. Gordon Liddy wishes the *A Team* star well before his match.

OPPOSITE: Piper and Mr. T put on the gloves and duke it out.

Football League players: Jumbo Jim Covert, Bill Fralic, Russ Francis, Ernie Holmes, Harvey Martin, and, of course, Chicago's beloved widebody, the star of "The Super Bowl Shuffle," William "The Refrigerator" Perry.

Perry was really the main attraction for this event. He was a huge star at the time, a three-hundred-twenty-pound lineman with a gap-toothed smile that could light up the Chicago skyline, and an ability to not only sack quarterbacks but score touchdowns as well. He had become a legitimate cult hero in the Windy City, and his presence gave *WrestleMania 2* added cachet.

In preparation for the event, we decided that it would be great to stage a mock weigh-in at a Chicago sports bar. But instead of a traditional scale, we used a big cattle scale, the kind farmers might use to weigh livestock. The weigh-in was about a month ahead of time, and we were able to get at least ninety percent of the participants into town for it. They were marched in, one by one, and asked to climb onto the scale. At the end, of course, we had several tons of "meat" on the scale, which made for a hell of a photo opportunity, and we made the local papers and the nightly news. It was great publicity and everyone seemed to have a good time.

One person who did not see any humor in this event was Big John Studd. Big John, who was listed at seven feet tall and about four hundred pounds, did not take part in the weigh-in. He arrived a few hours later and missed the festivities. That night there was a knock on my hotel room door. When I answered, Big John Studd was standing in front of me, filling the doorway, clearly seething about something. He proceeded to tell me that he didn't think it was proper for the weigh-in to have been held at a bar, because somehow that didn't fit with wrestling's "family image." But that was only the beginning of the tirade.

"You know, you're just a marketing guy," he said disgustedly. "And you're making a mockery of our business."

Before I had a chance to defend myself or the event, John looked behind me and saw a copy of the Chicago *Sun-Times* on the bed, folded open to an advertisement promoting *WrestleMania* and the weigh-in. Since we were trying to sell tickets in Chicago, it featured most prominently all of the football players who would be taking part—and *not* the wrestlers.

Big John blew up when he saw that. He grabbed me by my lapels, hoisted me off the ground, and slammed me against a wall. He looked down into my eyes and said, "You're

TOP: Mean Gene Okerlund interviews footballer William "The Refrigerator" Perry.

ABOVE: NFL stars gear up for the battle royal in Chicago.

an idiot! Don't you know who sells the tickets? It's us! It ain't them! We're the business, not them!"

I didn't even try to respond. Within a few seconds Big John loosened his grip and let me slide down the wall. Then he stormed out. Big John was an extreme example, of course, but his response was typical of the mind-set of many wrestlers of that period. They still weren't sure what they were, or what the company wanted them to be. Wrestlers? Athletes? Entertainers? Some combination of the three? The business was evolving, changing, and not everyone was ready to go along for the ride.

On the night of the event we brought in Clara Peller, a tiny, elderly woman who had gained a measure of fame for her role in a series of commercials for Wendy's restaurants. The plan was to have Clara step up to a microphone in the center of the ring and shout her trademark phrase, "Where's the beef?!" At that point twenty wrestlers and football players would march into the ring. Unfortunately, the mike went dead on Clara, so no one could hear her saying, not once, not twice, but three times, "Where's the beef?" Finally she was escorted away from ringside, and the battle royal went on as planned, with wrestlers and football players flying over the top rope for the better part of a half hour. The match ended when seven-foot-four Andre the Giant eliminated the last of his competitors, Bret "The Hit Man" Hart.

The plan called for Andre to receive a trophy from a local sponsor after the match, as the crowd waited for the Los Angeles portion of *WrestleMania* to begin on closed-circuit. But where does a five-hundred-pound giant go after a match? Anywhere he wants to go. Andre was a real gentleman, very nice and considerate of others, but sometimes he just did what he wanted to do. And on this night, he didn't feel like waiting around in the ring. So he walked out. I was waiting at the end of the runway, way in the back of the arena, holding the trophy, when I saw Andre approaching. As he drew near, the sponsor expressed concern.

"But I thought we were supposed to be in the ring."

The poor guy expected to go out and present Andre with a trophy, shake his hand, and get a nice pop from the crowd. "Come on," I said, and dragged the guy down the runway. We met Andre just outside the main arena, beyond the view of the audience. I quickly introduced the two of them. The man shook Andre's hand, congratulated him on his victory, and presented him with the trophy. Andre thanked him, took the trophy, stared at it for a moment, then flipped it over his shoulder. The trophy rattled across the floor and broke into several pieces as Andre walked away, leaving the bewildered sponsor in his wake.

TOP: Rocker Ozzy Osbourne with Captain Lou Albano.

ABOVE: Clara "Where's the Beef?!" Peller.

OVERLEAF: Federation Superstars tangle with NFL bonecrushers in battle royal.

Los Angeles The Los Angeles portion of *WrestleMania 2* featured Hulk Hogan, whose popularity was approaching a peak. "Hulkamania" was sweeping the land, and Hulk was telling his legions of little fans to "train, say your prayers, and eat your vitamins." With his neon yellow-and-red outfits, his long, flowing blond hair, and his massive physique, Hulk was as close to a living, breathing action figure as the world had ever seen.

Although LA featured an array of celebrities—including *Silver Spoons* star Ricky (later to become Rick) Schroeder, Los Angeles Dodgers manager Tommy Lasorda, tough-guy actor Robert Conrad, and late-night horror show host Elvira—the focus was on the wrestlers, particularly Hulk and his main event opponent, King Kong Bundy. Bundy and Hulk had spent months feeding and fueling a rivalry. They had traded victories and insults on a nightly basis. At *WrestleMania 2* they would settle their feud once and for all, in a timeless manner reserved for all truly great events: a steel cage match.

Hulk overcame both Bundy and interference from Bundy's bad-guy manager, Bobby "The Brain" Heenan, to retain the Federation title. And this really began a series of *WrestleMania*s in which Hulk was, in one way or another, involved in what happened to the championship belt. In that sense, *WrestleMania 2* raised the bar and demonstrated that the acquisition of the title belt was always going to be an important part of *WrestleMania*.

But the feeling coming out of this evening—despite the fact that we reached more than 300,000 people through closed-circuit and Pay-Per-View—was that it was less than a great event. The sum total was terrific, but each individual site was lacking. *WrestleMania 2* confirmed the company's belief in the integrity of the live event. I'm not talking about the integrity of the competition, but the integrity and the value of the product . . . the *show*. If you don't give fans something they really want to see when they're sitting a hundred feet from the ring, then why would anybody care at home? And *WrestleMania 2*, divided into three sites, did not deliver in each of those sites a product that met the lofty standards established by the World Wrestling Federation.

It was a valuable lesson. More than anything else, *WrestleMania 2* proved that the site was king.

LEFT: *WrestleMania 2* drew Tinseltown's finest, including rugged actor Robert Conrad; future *NYPD Blue* star Rick Schroeder and Zsa Zsa Gabor; baseball's Tommy Lasorda; and horror goddess Elvira (with Jesse Ventura).

OPPOSITE: Hulk Hogan opens up King Kong Bundy in their Los Angeles cage match.

WWF WRESTLEMANIA® III

World Wrestling Federation Title Match:

Hulk Hogan (Champion) vs. Andre the Giant

World Wrestling Federation Intercontinental Title Match:

Randy "Macho Man" Savage
(Champion—managed by Miss Elizabeth)
vs. Ricky "The Dragon" Steamboat
(with George "The Animal" Steele in his corner)

Retirement Match:

Rowdy Roddy Piper vs. Adorable Adrian Adonis

Six-Man Tag Team Match:

British Bulldogs & Tito Santana
vs. The Hart Foundation & Dangerous Danny Davis
(managed by Jimmy Hart)

Humiliation Match:

The Junk Yard Dog vs. King Harley Race
(managed by Bobby "The Brain" Heenan)

Jake "The Snake" Roberts (with Alice Cooper)
vs. Honky Tonk Man (managed by Jimmy Hart)

Billy Jack Haynes vs. Hercules Hernandez
(managed by Bobby "The Brain" Heenan)

Hillbilly Jim, Little Beaver & The Haiti Kid
vs. King Kong Bundy, Little Tokyo & Lord Littlebrook

Rougeau Brothers vs. The Dream Team (Valentine & Beefcake)

Koko B. Ware vs. The Natural Butch Reed (managed by Slick)

Can-Am Connection (Rick Martel & Tom Zenk)
vs. The Magnificent Muraco & Cowboy Bob Orton
(managed by Mr. Fuji)

In planning for WrestleMania III, Vince McMahon once again had a distinct vision: it had to be even bigger. This presented something of a problem, since *WrestleMania 2,* for all its problems, was undeniably huge. More than 47,000 people had witnessed the event in person. We had covered three time zones. How do you top that? Well, by putting on a better show, for starters. But that wasn't enough. In one of our earliest planning meetings we had decided that this version of *WrestleMania* would be *WrestleMania III,* with a Roman numeral, instead of *WrestleMania 3.* Other than the Super Bowl, no event had consistently dared to present itself as being worthy of this sort of designation. There was an implied importance, and even if it was mostly bluster, it was appropriate for our purposes. So, as we tried to come up with a catchphrase for the event, someone said, "Let's see, this one is going to be bigger, it's going to be better, it's going to be badder—"

Vince jumped in at that point, as he often did in these settings. "Stop right there," he said. He held a hand up in the air, as if to draw the words. "*WrestleMania III:* Bigger, Better, Badder."

And that was it. Everyone around the table nodded and smiled. Vince had hit upon the perfect slogan.

The next trick was to make good on the promise. Creating a *WrestleMania* that would be badder and better wasn't much of a concern. That, after all, is what we did. But bigger? That would be a challenge. Vince decided that

OPPOSITE: Hogan tries locking his arms around Andre in the main event.

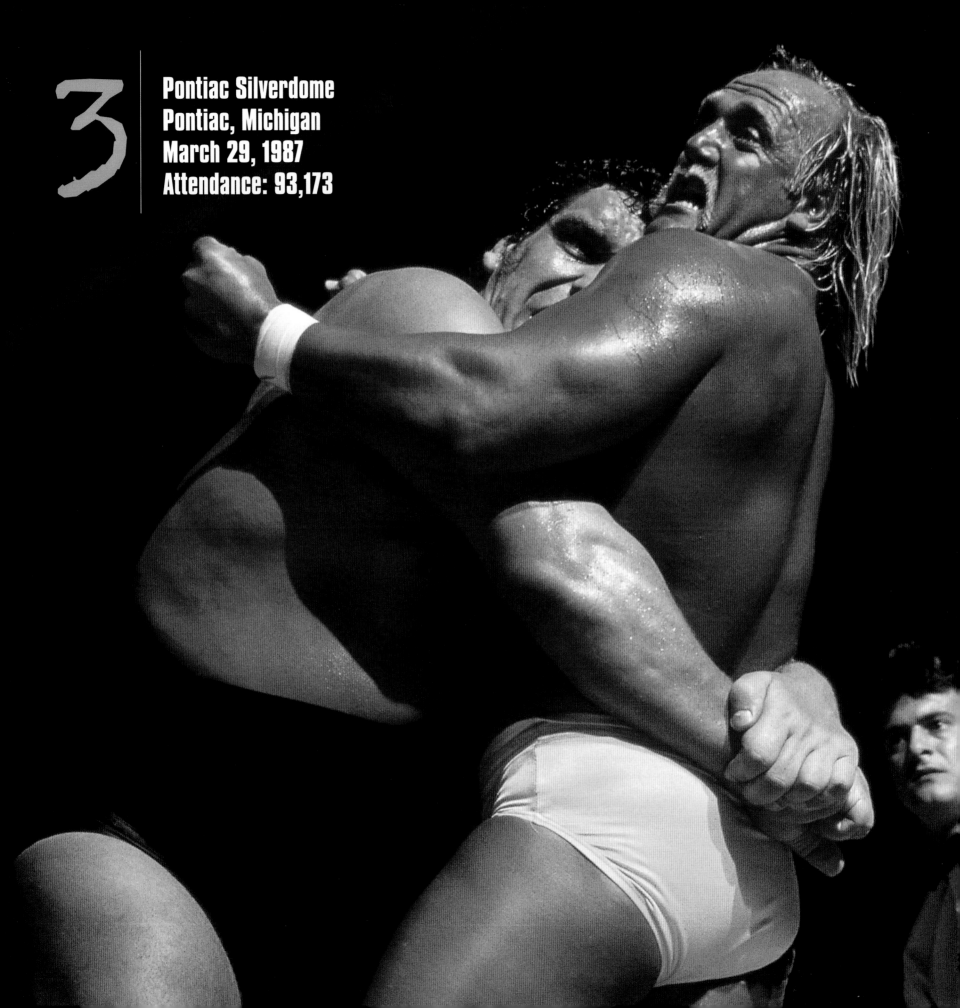

3 | **Pontiac Silverdome**
Pontiac, Michigan
March 29, 1987
Attendance: 93,173

the only way to create a bigger spectacle than the previous year's *WrestleMania* was to increase the live gate—without using more than one facility. That meant taking *Wrestle-Mania III* to a stadium. In 1987 there were fewer options than there are today, especially in the eastern half of the country, where the World Wrestling Federation has always had its strongest fan base. Theoretically, we could have selected a warm climate and an outdoor venue. But weather is always a risk in outdoor stadiums, and an event in the sunlight is not quite as dramatic.

It had to be a dome, and it didn't take long to settle on the Silverdome in Pontiac, Michigan, as the first choice. In fact, the decision was made at 2:00 A.M., when Vince picked up the telephone and called his event booker, Ed Cohen. Ed, of course, was sound asleep, so when the answering machine picked up, Vince began speaking in rapid-fire bursts into the phone: "Wake up! Wake up!" Vince wanted Ed on a plane first thing in the morning with a fifty-thousand-dollar check! He wanted the Silverdome for *WrestleMania*.

And he got it. The Silverdome had already been booked for a convention, but the Federation bought out the event and secured the facility. Now we were set. If all went well, we'd be able to put more than 90,000 fans in the building—an outrageous number of people for a single live event. But of course, when planning an event of this magnitude, things never go smoothly. There are always obstacles.

A Hot Ticket Based on our concern about the possibility of selling 60,000 tickets (which would have been an all-time wrestling record) and still having 30,000 empty seats, and thus having the event branded a "failure," it was decided to exclude the entire state of Michigan from Pay-Per-View access. This blackout was not exactly a popular move with some of our fans (to say nothing of the Pay-Per-View executives), but it seemed necessary. Despite the fact that we had a main event—Hulk Hogan versus Andre the Giant, perhaps the most promotable match of all time—we were entering new territory, and there was significant risk involved. But we didn't feel good about the blackout; in fact, we haven't blacked out an area since.

I first learned of the site for *WrestleMania III* in January, at the National Association of Television Program Executives convention in New Orleans. This was an annual event at which all television programming for the following year was sold. On Thursday, January 22, Vince and Hulk Hogan came to our booth to meet with television executives, shake some hands, pump the business. Following their appearance, I walked Hulk and Vince to their limo for the ride to the airport. When Vince told me that we were going to the Silverdome, I held out some hope that, by

WRESTLEMANIA III™

The World Wrestling Federation cordially invites you to experience WrestleMania III, live and in person, at the Pontiac Silverdome in Pontiac, Michigan, on March 29, 1987 at 4:00 p.m.

Since you have been part of the WrestleMania family, we have reserved two complimentary tickets in your name at our office, and we are anxious to send them out immediately.

If you would like to attend our super spectacular, please contact Basil DeVito or Toni Starson by Wednesday, March 11th. The phone number is 203-352-8620.

We look forward to hearing from you!

WWF
WORLD WRESTLING FEDERATION®

DATE
1987
GOOD ONLY FOR DATE INDICATED

NAME
RETURN TO STEVE TAYLOR

LOCATION
ALL LOCATIONS

TYPE
PHOTOGRAPHY

ACCESS
RINGSIDE

NOT GOOD FOR ADMISSION
® REGISTERED TRADEMARK OF
S, INC.

using curtains and other devices, we could configure the building in such a way that 40,000 or 50,000 might be capacity.

These were the thoughts running through my head as we walked down an access corridor outside the convention's main display area. Hulk—walking two or three steps ahead of me and Vince—was wearing red tights with the word "Hulkamania" printed down the side of each leg, tucked into cowboy boots. He wore a yellow Hulkamania bandanna and carried a Hulkamania leather gym bag. As we talked, it was clear that Vince was unmoved by ideas on capacity and configuration.

"We're going all the way," he said. "Find out what the record is for the largest indoor crowd in history—for *any* event. Then make sure we can put enough seats in the Silverdome to break it."

Then he paused and smiled.

"What do you think?"

I swallowed hard. "Well, Vince, to be honest . . . I'm scared to death."

With that, Hulk stopped, put down his bags, and turned to face us. He walked right up to me, not in a menacing way, but in a very serious way. He leaned down, put his nose a few inches from mine, and said in that sandpaper voice of his, "Ain't you heard who's in the main event, brother?"

That was the last time I voiced my concern out loud.

Immediately I flew to Michigan to begin the process of putting tickets on sale. The first step was a site survey. We went through a meeting with the executive staff of the Silverdome. We talked about how the event would work and discussed the logistics of installing four giant color television screens so that everyone in the building would be able to see the event. Engineers would have to be brought in to figure out how to safely hang these giant screens over

ABOVE: Women's legend, the Fabulous Moolah, displays King Harley Race's crown.

RIGHT: Bob Uecker, with Mary Hart, finally made it to "the front row."

the ring. Because the Silverdome's roof is translucent and air-supported, nothing can be affixed to it, so installing these screens was no small engineering feat. As usual, Vince decided that price would not be an issue. He wanted this to work. He wanted the largest indoor crowd in history, regardless of the cost.

So we walked the entire stadium, and finally Vince asked to be taken to the worst seat in the house.

"I want to make sure this person can see the screen," Vince said.

"That's right," someone added. "Even from the Uecker seats." We all laughed. This was a reference to Bob Uecker, the baseball-player-turned-broad-caster-turned-actor who was then starring in a popular series of Miller Lite commercials. Bob's character was always attending sporting events and claiming he belonged "in the front row," but invariably wound up in the cheap seats. And in part, that's why he was invited to be a guest announcer for *WrestleMania III*.

Most of us left the Silverdome that day and headed back home, but there was more work to do for Vince. We had the biggest venue in the country and we were going to draw the biggest crowd in history. To complete the picture, Vince wanted one of the biggest stars in Hollywood, a larger-than-life character. He wanted Arnold Schwarzenegger.

So, that very day, Vince McMahon, Dick Ebersol, and Jesse Ventura—former wrestler and future governor of Minnesota, as well as one of Arnold's co-stars in the movie *Predator*—climbed aboard a Learjet and flew to some remote jungle where Arnold was shooting his latest film. Unfortunately, they got to the area later than they intended, and the pilot spent considerable time circling and sweating, looking for a tiny landing strip in the fading light. Finally, Vince said, "Just put this thing down somewhere!" and the pilot found the airstrip with a hut as a control center and animals on the runway. He put the plane down safely and the unlikely trio went off in search of Arnold. They found him, spent the night, but ultimately weren't able to persuade him to participate in *WrestleMania III*. Instead, the lineup of celebrities included rock star Alice Cooper (a Motor City fixture), *Entertainment Tonight* host Mary Hart, the First Lady of Soul, Aretha Franklin (in keeping with a Motown theme), and Uecker. That roster, coupled with a potentially great main event involving Hulk and Andre, helped feed a ticket-buying frenzy that surprised almost everyone involved with *WrestleMania III*.

Tickets went on sale February 14. By March 2 we had sold 50,000 seats. By March 11 we had sold 74,000. And when we went to our production meeting on March 24, we had 90,000 tickets sold! At that point we cut off sales, because there was concern that we might oversell the building. By the time the final numbers came in from our remote outlets, the figure was 93,173. We had done the impossible: we had sold enough tickets to guarantee the largest indoor crowd in history. Bigger than the Rolling Stones concert at the Super-dome. Bigger than Super Bowl at the Silverdome. Bigger, even, than the Pope's appearance at the Silverdome several months later, which would draw 88,000. In fairness, it should be pointed out that for the Pope, they probably had to put in kneelers, which do take up a lot of space. Nevertheless, we outsold the Pope. That was nothing short of amazing.

OPPOSITE: Bob Uecker flexes with future governor Ventura; Jake "The Snake" Roberts and Alice Cooper; "Queen of Soul" Aretha Franklin.

RIGHT: Hulk Hogan dagger eyes his onetime ally Andre the Giant before their classic in the Detroit Silverdome.

Praying for Rain

We had sold more than 50,000 tickets when our television people came back to the office with a bit of distressing news: Because of the natural lighting in the Silverdome, the images on the giant screen wouldn't be visible until well after sundown, which was approximately 5:30 P.M., some ninety minutes after the start of *WrestleMania III*. There was, naturally, a great deal of concern about this, because we had always prided ourselves on being completely honest and straightforward with our fans, especially in terms of marketing and promotion. The idea that more than half the crowd wouldn't be able to tell what was going on in the ring was a major source of anxiety within the company in the weeks leading up to *Wrestle-Mania III*. We talked about moving the start time, but we were too far into the promotion for that. We talked about trying to place a giant tarpaulin—or hundreds of giant tarpaulins—over the roof of the Silverdome. We even talked about *painting* the roof of the Silverdome. None of that was going to happen.

Eventually we had a prolonged brainstorming session. There were more than a dozen people in the room—television executives, Pay-Per-View executives, operations staff. We went back and forth, throwing out ideas and suggestions that couldn't possibly work. Finally, somebody said, "What's the earliest time of day that the images will be clearly visible?" And the answer was, "Well, that depends on the day. If it's a dark, cloudy day, we'll be fine."

With that, Vince McMahon sat up in his seat, slapped the table with the palm of his hand, and said, "Done! It'll rain. End of discussion. Let's go."

We all sort of sat there for a moment, and after a short pause we realized that the meeting was in fact over. If you look back at the weather reports from that day, you'll see that it was cloudy with rain in Pontiac, Michigan. Not only were you able to see the early portion of the show on the big screens, but by starting in the gloaming and ending in the dark, a tremendous effect was created. In terms of staging, it was easily the most dramatic of all *WrestleManias*.

We did have one other challenge. The distance from the dressing room to the ring was more than fifty-five yards. Wrestlers are notorious for taking their time, especially once they're in front of the crowd, but even if they hurried to and from the ring, we'd have a five-hour event on entrances and exits alone. So we decided to transport the wrestlers to and from the ring in "scissor cars," four-wheel-drive vehicles that workers used to get around the

BELOW: Hillbilly Jim with his *WrestleMania III* tag team partners, Little Beaver and the Haiti Kid.

OPPOSITE: Hulk Hogan takes in the adulation of the crowd after defeating Andre.

LEFT: Hercules Hernandez batters Billy Jack Haynes with a chain.

BELOW: The Junkyard Dog sends King Harley Race to the mat.

RIGHT: Randy "Macho Man" Savage weathers a blow from Ricky "The Dragon" Steamboat.

Silverdome. It was quite a spectacle, really, these massive men hoisted above the height of the crowd as they glided toward the ring, like gladiators being carried into battle. The crowd absolutely loved it.

A Big Heart   Prior to *WrestleMania III*, Andre the Giant had undergone back surgery in England. During his rehabilitation, he lived with Vince in Greenwich, Connecticut. Andre had been in rough shape. He loved wrestling and performing perhaps more than anyone in the business. And the thought that wrestling might be taken away from him caused him to become depressed. But when Vince told him of the main-event idea for *WrestleMania III,* Andre was energized. He worked hard to strengthen his back. By the end of March he was far from healthy and still obviously in pain, but his spirits had improved substantially.

Andre, by this time, was being portrayed as evil personified. He was the seven-foot-four, five-hundred-pound bad guy threatening the ultimate good guy: Hulk Hogan. That, in essence, was the story line. The day before the event we had our regular production meeting, and at the end of the meeting Vince paused and said, "One more thing. Tomorrow night I want everybody associated with the World Wrestling Federation to be in the arena, watching this match. And anyone who leaves before the match is over might as well keep right on walking."

Vince clearly understood what this match meant to Andre, and to Hulk, and to the business. The fact that Andre the Giant was going to put Hulk over was, in Vince's eyes, an act of great courage and selflessness. The speculation surrounding the match was that Hulk Hogan was going to body slam Andre the Giant. Now, I don't know whether Andre really weighed five hundred pounds (which was the way he was promoted), but I do know that he was a giant of a man, and no one—not even Hulk Hogan—was going to pick him up off his feet unless he was willing to cooperate. Hulk and Andre had not discussed the match at all, so, in the last twenty-four hours, Hulk talked to Vince on a number of occasions and asked for reassurance that "The Boss," as everyone called Andre, was really willing to do this in a match.

Usually things are done differently. The basics of the match are in place further in advance. But on this occasion, the day before the match, Hulk still wasn't sure just how Andre was going to handle himself in the ring. And Andre was a unique guy. In much the same way that the wrestlers liked to keep the celebrities on edge during *WrestleMania*, I suspect Andre was probably playing his own little mind game with Hulk.

On the day of the event, everything worked out perfectly. The sky was cloudy and the screens were clear. In addition to the more than 90,000 fans in the Silverdome, several million more watched at home on Pay-Per-View or at closed-circuit outlets. Aretha Franklin sang a beautiful version of "America the Beautiful" in front of her largest audience. As the first match began and the crowd cheered so loudly that the Silverdome shook, Vince's step-mother looked skyward and said through tear-filled eyes, "Vincent, can you believe what the kid is doing? Can you believe it?"

Somewhere, of course, Vincent J. McMahon was surely smiling, for *WrestleMania III* was, by any standard, an overwhelming success. A record-setting crowd, an event worthy of the setting. In the main event, the match went back and forth as expected, with Hulk twice trying unsuccessfully to lift Andre off the mat. The crowd, despite its size and distance from the ring, was as mesmerized as any crowd I had ever seen. Neither Hulk nor Andre possessed tremendous agility or technical wrestling skill. But they were showmen,

and on this night they put on the show of their lives. When, finally, Hulk hoisted Andre into the air and over his head, the crowd fell briefly silent, as if not quite able to believe what was happening. As the giant crashed to the canvas with a great *THUD!* a roar went up from the crowd. It was pandemonium! Hulk covered Andre and walked off with the World Wrestling Federation championship belt, and one of the greatest nights in the history of sports-entertainment came to an end.

WRESTLEMANIA IV

World Wrestling Federation Championship Tournament:

Fourteen-Man Single Elimination Event Featuring:
Hulk Hogan, Andre the Giant, Million Dollar Man Ted
DiBiase, Hacksaw Jim Duggan, Don Muraco, Dino Bravo,
Ricky "The Dragon" Steamboat, Greg "The Hammer"
Valentine, Randy "Macho Man" Savage, Butch Reed,
Bam Bam Bigelow, One Man Gang, Jake "The Snake"
Roberts and Ravishing Rick Rude

World Wrestling Federation Intercontinental Title Match:

Honky Tonk Man (Champion—managed by Jimmy Hart)
vs. Brutus "The Barber" Beefcake

World Wrestling Federation Tag Team Title Match:

Strike Force (Champions)
vs. Demolition (managed by Mr. Fuji)

Six-Man Tag Team Match:

British Bulldogs & Koko B. Ware
vs. The Islanders
(managed by Bobby "The Brain" Heenan)

Grudge Match:

Ultimate Warrior vs. Hercules

Twenty-Man Over-the-Top-Rope Battle Royal:

Featuring: Sam Houston, Ken Patera, Brian Blair,
Jumping Jim Brunzell, Ray Rougeau, Jacques Rougeau,
Hillbilly Jim, Junk Yard Dog, Bad News Brown,
Dangerous Danny Davis, George "The Animal" Steele,
King Harley Race, Bret "Hit Man" Hart, Jim "The Anvil"
Neidhart, Sika, Outlaw Ron Bass, Paul Roma, Jim Powers,
Nikolai Volkoff and Boris Zhukov

It has been said of the World Wrestling Federation that they don't play well with other children. And that's probably true. We have a very specific way of doing things, and it doesn't always mesh well with the traditional corporate world. Dick Glover, who came to the company about the same time that I did, as director of new business (Dick is a very smart man who has since gone on to become head of business at ABC/Disney.com), once made an interesting observation about the folly of market research. "Our best research," he said, "is firmly embedded in Vince McMahon's guts, and it's hard to go away from that."

He was right. So many of the decisions that contributed to the World Wrestling Federation's incredible growth began with Vince simply saying, "Let's give it a try," or words to that effect. He worked on intuition, and he was utterly fearless. That attitude was nothing if not infectious.

So, as we began preparing for the fourth edition of *WrestleMania*, we were all searching for a way to make it unique, to somehow improve upon the spectacular event of 1987. This was no small task, considering how high the bar had been raised. We couldn't have a bigger crowd. That just wasn't possible. And the idea that the headlining match itself could be better . . . well, that didn't seem likely, either. In truth, we seemed to have bumped up against the ceiling.

RIGHT: The World Wrestling Federation rolled the dice by holding *WrestleMania IV* at Trump Plaza.

OPPOSITE: At the end of the night, Randy "Macho Man" Savage was anointed champion.

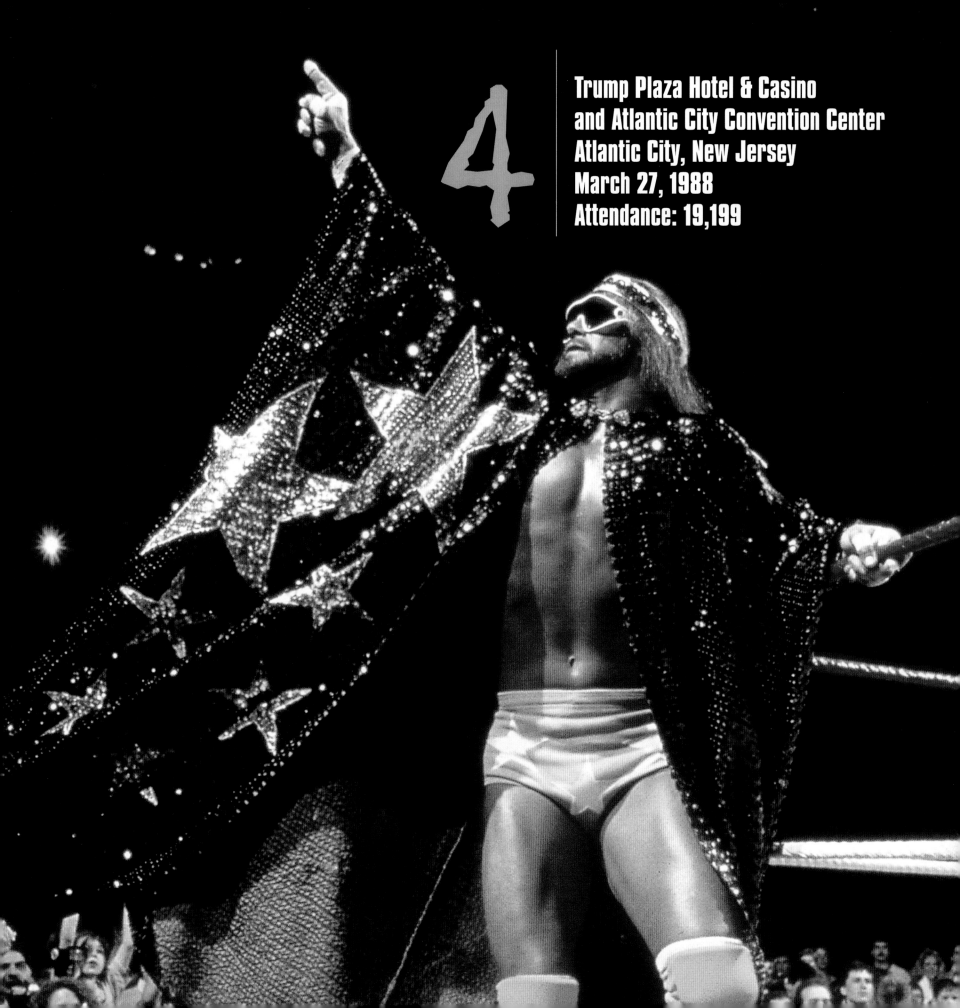

4

Trump Plaza Hotel & Casino
and Atlantic City Convention Center
Atlantic City, New Jersey
March 27, 1988
Attendance: 19,199

In January, though, during a business trip to Atlantic City, the ceiling moved. I was part of a panel discussion on the marketing of casino special events. Among the people on the dais was a man named Mark Grossinger Etess, who was president of Trump Plaza Hotel and Casino. Mark was a very smart, impressive guy, summa cum laude from Cornell, and as part of the Grossinger family, had been in the hospitality business pretty much his entire life. After the event Mark approached me and said, "You know, Basil, I think we ought to talk about bringing *WrestleMania* to Trump Plaza."

I was flattered but skeptical. "Mark, it's nice of you to say that, but I'm not sure that we appeal to your audience. You want gamblers, high rollers, like you get for a boxing match. And I don't think *WrestleMania* will attract the kind of crowd you want. That's not necessarily our core audience."

Mark looked at me and smiled. In the next five minutes he proceeded to summarize my business, his business, and the entire plan. I don't know whether he had mapped this out ahead of time, or if it simply came to him on the spur of the moment, but he clearly knew what he was talking about.

"You're right," he said. "But that's not what I mean. There's a whole level of player, a whole level of Trump customer, who we can't bring to a Mike Tyson fight. There are a lot of people who would love to come to Trump Plaza, watch an event, play some blackjack, stay overnight. They aren't necessarily high rollers, but they are successful businessmen, and they're in business for themselves in South Jersey and Philly. They'd like to bring their wives and kids to Atlantic City for the weekend and have a good time. This will give them the chance."

I could tell where he was going, and I liked the sound of it.

"Your event is on Palm Sunday, right?" Mark asked.

"Yeah."

"Well, that's not a great weekend for us. Very quiet. *Wrestle-Mania* would make it a better weekend. I have customers who would love to come down, but you'll have to expand your event. You've got to make it a full weekend and create events for the families and kids so that the guys will have time to play the tables. That way everybody has a good time."

In that brief conversation, Mark sold me on the idea of bringing *WrestleMania IV* to Atlantic City. He also sold me on the idea of creating what today has become *WrestleMania* FanFest. He even came up with the name. Over subsequent weeks we got together and discussed various activities that would not only make *WrestleMania IV* more of a family event, but extend the life of the event over the course of a full weekend, much as the NCAA does with the Final Four. We'd have a 5K run on Saturday morning, a carnival-type party on Saturday afternoon featuring autograph sessions with many of the World Wrestling Federation superstars, and a big party in the Trump Ballroom with our celebrity guests on Saturday night.

"You create these events," Mark said, "you execute them . . . and we'll pay for it all."

Mark even suggested a Sunday morning brunch with the wrestlers. "Call it 'Bacon, Bagels and Biceps,'" he said. And that's what we called it. In fact, out of respect for Mark, that's still the only name it's ever been called. You see, in October 1993 Mark and two other executives from the Trump organization died in a helicopter crash while traveling from New York to Atlantic City. I had attended a press conference with him that morning at the Plaza Hotel in New York. Mark had just started Trump Sports and Entertainment, and he acknowledged having created the business with Titan Sports, the parent company of the World Wrestling Federation, in mind. "If we can only do it half as good as you guys," he said. Hours later he climbed into a helicopter, and I never spoke with him again. Mark was the brightest young marketing executive I've ever met. More important, he was a good family man and a great dad. He was admired and respected by all who knew him, and he's been missed.

Million-Dollar Show

When I returned to the office after my trip to Atlantic City, I was pretty pumped up. I went to Vince and related Mark's pitch, and he liked the idea. As it turned out, although most people never realized it, we did improve on *WrestleMania III* in at least a couple significant ways. First, we sold the event to a record 600,000 homes on Pay-Per-View. Second, because the top-priced ticket was one hundred fifty dollars, we were able to surpass the live-gate revenue for *WrestleMania III,* even though there were only 18,900 seats at the Atlantic City Convention Center.

The show itself also was unusual. For the first time, the Federation championship was vacant heading into *WrestleMania*. Andre the Giant had taken the belt from Hulk Hogan in early February with a victory during an event that was telecast live during prime time on NBC. Afterward,

ABOVE: The championship tournament featured the most celebrated names in the World Wrestling Federation.

BELOW: A five-kilometer run on the Atlantic City boardwalk added to the event's festive mood.

though, Andre, who was now deeply immersed in the role of villain, tried to surrender the belt, in exchange for a payoff, to Ted DiBiase, the "Million Dollar Man." But, of course, if you read the World Wrestling Federation rule book, you will see quite clearly that when a champion surrenders the title, it cannot simply be given to another individual; rather, it reverts to the Federation. So the decision was made to create a tournament that would be played out, in its entirety, at *WrestleMania IV*. The winner would be crowned the new champion.

Although this format was unique, it was not without risk. Nothing like this had been attempted at *WrestleMania*, and there was no guarantee that it would work. Any concerns, however, were laid to rest on February 22, at a press conference in New York, featuring Andre, Hulk, and Donald Trump. The atmosphere was electric, and we got some great publicity out of it. In the next few days we began selling tickets like crazy. It took less than five weeks to break our live-gate and Pay-Per-View records.

I'd Like to Buy a Vowel
Since *WrestleMania IV* was at Trump Plaza, and Donald Trump naturally was one of the men primarily responsible for making that happen, it seemed to make sense to go with a theme reflecting the lifestyles of the rich and famous. So, who better to present the championship belt than Robin Leach, host of the television show *Lifestyles of the Rich and Famous*? The other celebrities invited to take part were Gladys Knight, who would sing "America the Beautiful"; Bob Uecker, simply because he had done such a wonderful job the previous year; and Vanna White, the glamorous card-turning hostess of the hit game show *Wheel of Fortune*. Vanna was at the peak of her popularity around this time, and she was wonderful to work with.

TOP: Bob Uecker made a triumphant return to the ring.

CENTER: Card turner Vanna White played spin doctor before the show.

LEFT: Gladys Knight stirred the crowd with her rendition of "America the Beautiful."

Looking Good

The World Wrestling Federation did a great job of transforming the site into the perfect venue for *WrestleMania IV,* and the Trump organization did everything possible at the hotel to make everyone feel important. The Atlantic City Convention Center, which was an old, dank building, was dressed up and made to look very appealing with lighting and decorations. When you walked through the

Newly minted champion Randy "Macho Man" Savage addresses his legions.

Trump Plaza casino, instead of hearing the usual disembodied voices pumped through the public address system, you'd hear Hulk Hogan or Randy Savage saying, "Hey, don't forget this is *WrestleMania* weekend, oooh yeah!" or "Whatcha gonna do when Hulkamania runs wild on you?!" All the tent cards in the restaurants had a World Wrestling Federation theme. If you made a phone call and were placed on hold, you'd hear Federation theme music and promos. Chocolate bars bearing the company logo were distributed to guests. All of our performers and staff were invited to eat in the casino's employee cafeteria, so it was nothing to go down there and see Jake the Snake or Brutus "The Barber" Beefcake sitting next to a couple of blackjack dealers or other Trump staffers. It was an odd experience, but at the same time comforting. No one has ever treated us any better than the people at Trump Plaza. They handled every problem gracefully, no matter how unusual.

I remember Mark Etess approaching me in the casino the day of the event and saying, "You've got to do me a favor."

"Sure, you name it."

He smiled and handed me two tickets to *WrestleMania IV.* "Can you take care of these?"

"What do you want me to do with them?"

"I don't know. I was standing out by the front desk and Brutus Beefcake came up to me, put his arm around me, and said, 'Hey, pal . . . sell these for whatever you can get and bring me the money backstage, all right?'"

Brutus apparently mistook the president of Trump Plaza for the concierge. Of course, this is the same man who once walked into a locker room holding open a magazine featuring a revealing pictorial of his girlfriend and proclaimed, "Hey . . . look at this!" That's what you got with Brutus.

Jake the Snake was a handful, too, and in fact he was the instigator of one of the more interesting and memorable events at *WrestleMania IV*. Jake always carried a live, twelve-foot python into the ring—that's how he got his nickname. Jake had a great deal of control over the python. It never got loose. Nevertheless, the idea that he carried this snake around with him frightened a lot of people, including some of his co-workers. Part of the deal with Jake's character—one of the things that made him both appealing and somewhat creepy—was his fondness for laying the snake on top of his fallen victims. In promoting matches, it really wasn't much of a stretch for some of the guys in the company to say, quite convincingly, "I don't like snakes." This held true for the average fan, as well. When Jake came out of the ring after a match, he always held the snake out in front of him. With a flick of the wrist he could make the snake dart one way or the other. It was only going to go a foot or two, but that was enough to make people scream and jump back. Even though he had never lost control of the snake, and there had never been an accident, there was just enough uncertainty to give Jake's performances a legitimate edge.

Just ask Ivana Trump.

Ivana, who was then Donald Trump's wife, was seated at ringside as Jake made his way back through the crowd after wrestling to a draw with Ravishing Rick Rude in their first-round match. Chief Jay Strongbow used to say that the two most important moves in wrestling were "coming and going," because those are the times when a wrestler has complete control over what he's doing. Coming out of the ring, Jake decided to do a little preening and get some additional airtime. Instead of walking straight back to the dressing room, he walked clockwise around the ring, and as he passed Ivana and Donald, the snake made a quick little move in their direction. It probably didn't get within a foot or two of them, but that was close enough to startle Ivana. She jumped back and a glass of wine got spilled all over her dress.

To say Ivana was not pleased would be an understatement. As Jake continued his post-match strut, security guards whisked Ivana out the door and gave her a ride back to

Trump Plaza, which was no more than three hundred yards away. The next day one of the security guys told me what had happened afterward.

"Man, you guys don't make it easy," he said. "When I was getting her into the limo she looked me right in the eye and said, 'Why didn't you shoot the damn snake?' She was serious, too."

A New Champ

A New Champ Although Hulk Hogan and Andre the Giant had been the biggest stars in the World Wrestling Federation, they were eliminated early in the featured tournament at *WrestleMania IV*. By this time we knew that Hulk was interested in branching out and working in movies, and Andre was not in the best of health. The stage was set for a new champion to emerge, and that person was Randy

Favorites Andre and Hogan were eliminated early in the tournament.

Savage—the "Macho Man." With Hulk working his corner (to counter the presence of Andre in the corner of Ted DiBiase), Randy eliminated the Million Dollar Man to become the new Federation champion. And afterward, in a gesture of brotherhood and support, Hulk Hogan formally presented the belt to Randy. It was a wonderful photo opportunity, one of those moments that remains frozen in time—the passing of the belt from champion to champion, so that the fans would immediately get behind Randy and accept him as champion, because, after all, it was okay with Hulk.

Interestingly, Randy's picture had appeared on the cover of the World Wrestling Federation magazine, with the word "champion" above his head, two days before *WrestleMania IV*. The magazine had mistakenly left the distribution warehouse early! This was back in the days when, although we had adopted the term "sports-entertainment" to describe what we were doing, the world hadn't really grasped the concept. Professional wrestling existed in sort of an uncomfortable gray area. The entire office was depressed about it when the issue first came out. Here we were, seventy-two hours before the event, embarrassing ourselves by making this mistake. But Vince said, "Just keep working." And that's what we did. The event went off without a ripple of controversy. On Monday I got a call from a reporter in Philadelphia who had a copy of the magazine.

"Hah!" he said. "I got you!"

"How's that?"

"If Randy Savage just became champion on Sunday, how is it that I saw a copy of your magazine, with him listed as champion, on Friday? Explain that. It's all fixed. You guys know what's going to happen."

I didn't get angry. I didn't take the bait. Instead, very calmly, I said to the reporter, "You know what? Friday you had a hell of a story. Today you've got a mere coincidence."

ABOVE: A victorious Savage hoists Miss Elizabeth on his shoulders.

OPPOSITE: The Macho Man is congratulated by the Hulkster.

WrestleMania V

World Wrestling Federation Title Match:
Randy "Macho Man" Savage (Champion) vs. Hulk Hogan

World Wrestling Federation Intercontinental Title Match:
Ultimate Warrior (Champion)
vs. Ravishing Rick Rude (managed by Bobby "The Brain" Heenan)

Jake "The Snake" Roberts vs. Andre the Giant (with special guest referee Big John Studd)

World Wrestling Federation Tag Team Title Match:
Demolition (Champions—managed by Mr. Fuji)
vs. Powers of Pain

Red Rooster vs. Bobby "The Brain" Heenan

Hacksaw Jim Duggan vs. Bad News Brown

Hart Foundation
vs. Greg "The Hammer" Valentine & Honky Tonk Man

Rugged Ronnie Garvin vs. Dino Bravo

Strike Force vs. Brain Busters

Brutus "The Barber" Beefcake
vs. Million Dollar Man Ted DiBiase

Bushwhackers vs. The Fabulous Rougeaus

Blue Blazer vs. Mr. Perfect

The Rockers vs. The Twin Towers

Hercules vs. King Haku
(managed by Bobby "The Brain" Heenan)

Plus a Special Piper's Pit featuring Rowdy Roddy Piper with his guests Brother Love & Morton Downey Jr.

It had always been an unspoken rule

that *WrestleMania* would move to a different site each year. We knew that we could promote the event in almost any city, and by not putting down roots we had an opportunity to increase the popularity of the World Wrestling Federation and influence different parts of the country in a way that almost no other major athletic or entertainment spectacle event could do. The Super Bowl, as an example, is mostly corporate now, so they limit the selection to a handful of potential sites. They typically rotate from one domed stadium to another, completing the entire cycle within just a few years. The plan for *WrestleMania* was to keep moving, to enter a new city each spring and promote the best event possible, thereby cultivating new fans and new business relationships.

In 1989, though, that plan was temporarily shelved. The Trump organization had done such a great job with *WrestleMania IV* that it was hard to imagine a better host for the event. They wanted us back, and we were willing to consider a return engagement. In listening to their pitch, and in recalling the previous year's success, we realized that Trump had a very clear understanding of our needs and the ways in which *WrestleMania* could be taken to a national audience. They were able to provide the type of growth and promotion that changed our minds—they even found a way to add another 2,000 seats so that we could set the all-time attendance record at the Atlantic City Convention Center: more than 20,000 people. Trump Plaza also held closed-circuit parties at their other properties in Atlantic City because the demand for tickets was so great

OPPOSITE: Savage clamps a headlock on his "former friend" Hogan.

5

Trump Plaza Hotel & Casino and
Atlantic City Convention Center
Atlantic City, New Jersey
April 2, 1989
Attendance: 20,369

that they were unable to accommodate all of their VIPs and invited guests. Even though these people could not be in the arena, they were able to watch the event on a big screen and enjoy first-class amenities. The number of Pay-Per-View households grew by more than 200,000. In other words, in many ways, by returning to Atlantic City we not only avoided the potential trap of becoming stale, we actually raised the bar even higher.

ABOVE: Run DMC rocked the house in Atlantic City.

RIGHT: The show featured trash talking talk-show host Morton Downey Jr.

A Shift in Attitude

In retrospect, *WrestleMania V* can be seen as the beginning of a change for the Federation, a shift to a more diverse product. There had always been a patriotic, apple-pie kind of image associated with the World Wrestling Federation, embodied most obviously in the person of Hulk Hogan. Hulk routinely dispatched villains who often were stereotypical enemies of the free world, fascist caricatures such as the Iron Sheik and Nikolai Volkoff. By the time of *WrestleMania V,* though, the lines were blurring just a bit. Room was being made for the antihero, the performer whose character was more gray than black or white. The business was becoming louder, bolder, more in-your-face. So it's no coincidence that *WrestleMania V* reflected this change. Jesse Ventura, who had hung up his tights and become a highly entertaining announcer, served as a balance to the beloved and more laid-back Gorilla Monsoon. Instead of huggable celebrities such as Vanna White and Bob Uecker, *WrestleMania V* featured the rap group Run-DMC and controversial talk show host Morton Downey Jr., whose overtly confrontational manner (he was instigating fistfights long before anyone had ever heard of Jerry Springer) made him the celebrity you loved to hate in the 1980s. The event also featured a guest appearance by Jimmy "Superfly" Snuka, who, a decade earlier, had been one of the World Wrestling Federation's most popular and edgy stars.

To help broaden the appeal of the show, Sean Mooney was positioned as a roving reporter. Sean was a young, talented guy with a traditional sports background who had recently joined our company. For the first time, a reporter was placed in the audience at *WrestleMania,* and his job was to roam about and interview celebrities and wrestling fans.

Sean was very new to all of this, and even though he was clearly talented, he was nervous about being out of his element. Compounding his anxiety was the fact that although his boss, Vince McMahon, is a very dynamic and forceful television producer, and much of what happens at *WrestleMania* is very tightly scripted, there is also an understanding that a certain amount of spontaneity makes the program complete. When a host or reporter is sent out into the audience to interview or interact, it's not completely scripted. There is a direction about the kind of questions that should be asked, but really it's up to the talent to make it entertaining.

Sean was a solid host who could handle a straight interview, but interviewing Donald Trump at *WrestleMania* is different. One of my jobs was to orchestrate these situations, to help the talent find the potential interview candidate and move them into close proximity of each other. For whatever reason—whether it was because he was in unfamiliar territory, or because he was suddenly aware that he was working in front of a vast worldwide Pay-Per-View audience—interviewing Donald Trump suddenly became a horrible, nerveracking experience for Sean. He stumbled trough the interview, mispronouncing Donald Trump's name and making numerous mistakes, and to this day it stands as one of the worst interviews in the history of *WrestleMania*. He just didn't get the job done. Afterward, Sean felt absolutely devastated. He was backstage while the event was still going on, and he was completely distraught. I remember a brief interlude, no more than thirty seconds, in which he was being admonished by Vince McMahon. As Vince spoke, he chastised Sean not for blowing the interview and doing what really was bad television, but for blowing it because of nervousness. Vince couldn't understand how someone with talent had let his emotions get in the way of a good performance.

ABOVE: The Donald and The Hulkster form a tag team.

BELOW: Sean Mooney interviews Strike Force: Rick Martell (left) and Tito Santana (right).

"Go back out there and have some fun!" Vince said. "Don't you understand? This is entertainment. This is *fun*. What have you got to be nervous about?"

Sean nodded, returned to his post, and did a commendable job the rest of the night.

As did Roddy Piper, who turned the tables on Morton Downey Jr. during a segment of "Piper's Pit," Roddy's version of a talk show. Morton Downey's success—and it had soared seemingly overnight—stemmed largely from his penchant for agitating guests. He would

Rowdy Roddy Piper
shuts up Downey
with a fire
extinguisher
blast.

bring people of vastly different viewpoints together and goad them into fighting—sometimes with each other, sometimes with their host. Regardless of what you thought of Morton Downey Jr. or his act, it was obvious to those of us in the business that he was the type of celebrity who understood exactly what we were doing at *WrestleMania*. Some celebrities "get it," some celebrities "don't get it." The ones who haven't a clue as to what we're doing tend to be a challenge at *Wrestle-Mania*; at best, they provide lackluster entertainment. To be honest, we didn't know what to expect from Morton Downey Jr., but he absolutely "got it," and he was great to work with.

One of Downey's signatures was his cigarette smoking. He always had a cigarette in his hand, always smoked on the air, even while he was doing interviews. Sometimes, in the heat of an argument, he'd even blow smoke into the face of his guests. So it was Downey's idea to use that trademark as a way to incite Roddy Piper. The two got into a fight and began screaming at each other. When Morton Downey Jr. blew smoke at Roddy, Roddy responded by picking up a fire extinguisher and spraying its contents directly into Downey's face. The crowd loved it, of course. It was great theater! And it worked because Morton Downey Jr. was not only *willing* to play the comic foil, but actually *suggested* it.

Friends and Rivals

WrestleMania V featured a record fourteen matches, including Big John Studd officiating a battle between Jake the Snake and Andre the Giant; but the one that drew the most attention, the one people really wanted to see, was the grudge match between reigning champion Randy Savage and the former champion Hulk Hogan. The two characters had formed a friendship that was cemented at *WrestleMania IV* with the passing of the belt from Hulk to Randy. And they subsequently had worked together as a tag team known as the "Mega-Powers." But a feud had erupted in the months leading up to *WrestleMania V,* the roots of which could be traced back to the celebration following *WrestleMania IV,* when Randy and Hulk were in the ring together, along with Randy's manager, Miss Elizabeth. In Randy's estimation, photos and videotape showed Hulk getting a bit too friendly with Miss Elizabeth. Randy's character was extraordinarily jealous when it came to Miss Elizabeth, so a rift in the Mega-Powers naturally developed.

Making this story line particularly compelling was the fact that Randy and Miss Elizabeth were in actuality married, and Randy was indeed an extremely protective, if not jealous, man. That, to me, is one of the reasons so many of the World Wrestling Federation soap-opera story lines work so well and resonate with our fans: the line between reality and fantasy is sometimes blurred.

Great care is always taken in our organization to treat talent in a very professional manner, just as you would treat any other talented celebrity, whether it's an actor, a singer, an artist . . . whatever. So Randy had a comfort level with those of us in the organization who had been around for a few years. It was not unusual, during a photo shoot or while being ushered through a crowd, for Randy to be very concerned about people touching Elizabeth. There were perhaps a half-dozen of us who could put an arm around Elizabeth while guiding her through an airport terminal without incurring the wrath of Randy Savage. If a security guard or some other individual tried to touch Elizabeth, even in a purely benign way, Randy would not be a happy person. When we set up photo opportunities for guests at Trump Plaza, we had to go to great lengths to make sure that the guest did not put his arm around Elizabeth. If the photo involved Randy, Elizabeth, and

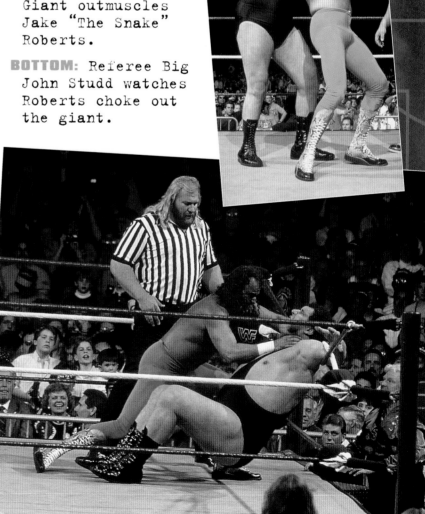

RIGHT: Andre the Giant outmuscles Jake "The Snake" Roberts.

BOTTOM: Referee Big John Studd watches Roberts choke out the giant.

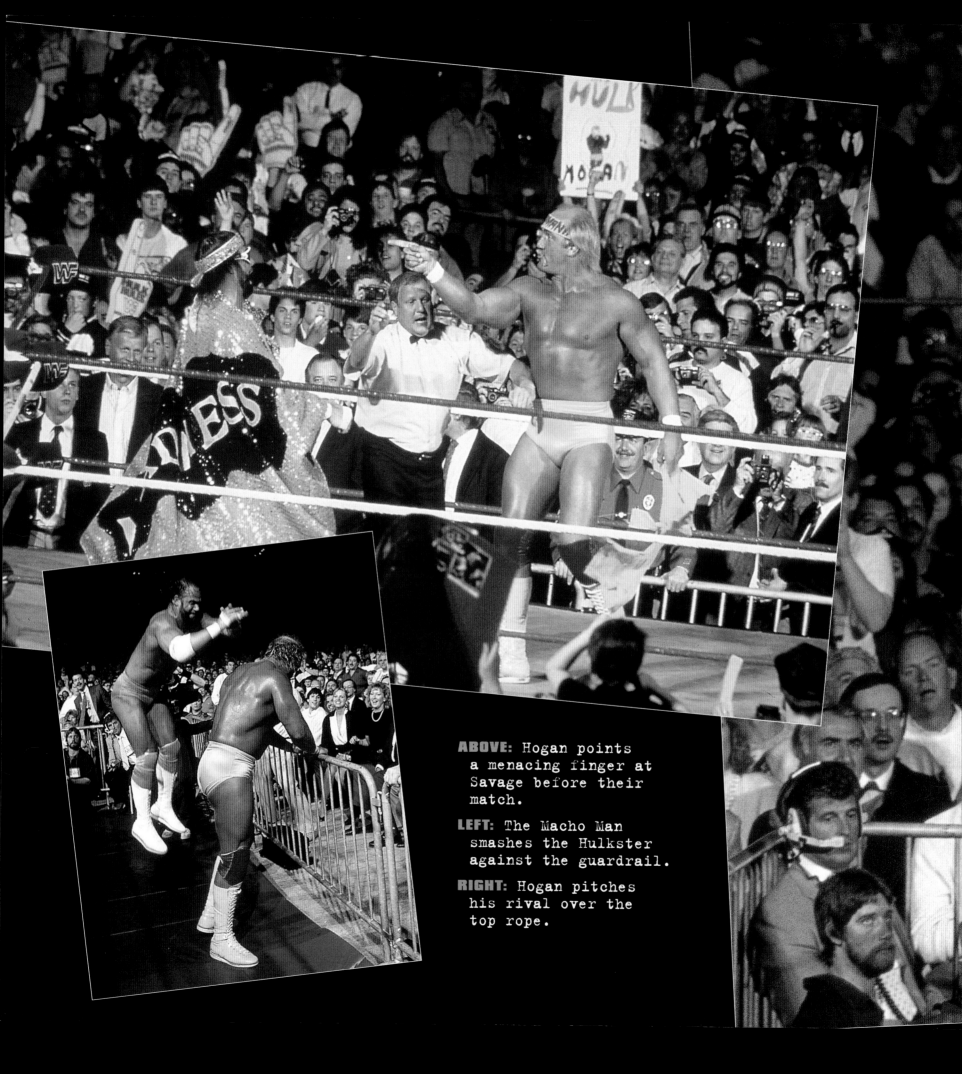

ABOVE: Hogan points a menacing finger at Savage before their match.

LEFT: The Macho Man smashes the Hulkster against the guardrail.

RIGHT: Hogan pitches his rival over the top rope.

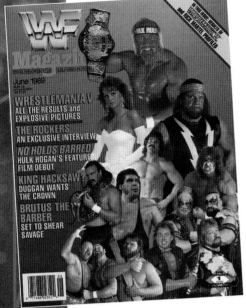

another person, Randy was much more comfortable if he was in the middle. So there was this part of Randy's personality that actually existed, and it made for a very energetic promotion and event. Although in reality there was no bad blood between Randy and Hulk, Randy could use this situation as motivation for a great performance.

In fact, they both performed brilliantly. The image of the Macho Man, in his burnt-orange trunks, and Hulk Hogan, decked out in electric yellow and red, to me represents a signpost in the history of the World Wrestling Federation and *WrestleMania.* Gone were the days of nonathletic-looking men in simple black or white. In their place were two well-tanned, well-defined performers wearing bright and bold uniforms. Hulk was a spectacular physical specimen, close to six-feet-seven, three hundred pounds. Randy was simply a gifted athlete—a former minor league baseball player who worked hard to keep himself in shape. He'd been a major league prospect as a catcher, and after separating his throwing shoulder he came back as a first baseman. Together they really combined to redefine pro-fessional wrestling. Their championship match was not only dramatic, but exceptionally ath-letic—a lot of back-and-forth, flying off the top rope, that sort of thing. There were several points when it looked as though either man might win, especially when Randy drove Hulk to his knees and prepared to deliver what appeared to be a devastating punch to Hulk's face. But Hulk just shook it off, and in that moment the crowd at the Atlantic City Convention Center came fully to life. Today we see The Rock whip fans into a frenzy simply by lifting an eyebrow; in 1989, with Hulkamania still gripping the land, Hulk Hogan could elicit the same response by wiggling his fingers. The idea was that Hulk drew his energy, his strength, from the fans. When Hulk simply shook his head after taking the best blow Randy had to give, the fans went wild. The remainder of the match followed a predictable but nonetheless thrilling arc, with Hulk charging back from the brink of defeat and reclaiming the championship.

Afterward, of course, Hulk marched around the ring, holding the belt aloft as his theme music—a power ballad typical of the 1980s called "Real American"—roared through the convention center's sound system. He went into his flex routine, posing and strutting and milking the moment for all it was worth. The crowd couldn't seem to get enough of it, so Hulk just kept the show going. Even today I get goose bumps thinking about it. The post-match celebration was the best part of Hulk's performance, frankly, and that's saying a lot when you consider just how compelling the match had been. Hulk was at his absolute best that night. He performed great, he looked great. That entire match, I believe, was the closest the World Wrestling Federation has ever come to delivering a perfect show—by all criteria.

And even though we didn't know it at the time, it was also the last time we would see the image of the invincible Hulk Hogan. It was, in effect, the end of an era.

ABOVE: *Wrestle-Mania V* sig-naled the end of the entity known as the Mega-Powers.

OPPOSITE: Once again, Hulk Hogan emerged on top of the mountain in the Federation.

WrestleMania® VI

World Wrestling Federation Title Match:
Hulk Hogan (Federation Champion)
vs. Ultimate Warrior (IC Champion)

World Wrestling Federation Tag Team Title Match:
Colossal Connection (Champions)
vs. Demolition

Mixed Tag Team Match:
The American Dream Dusty Rhodes & Sapphire
vs. Macho King Randy Savage & Queen Sherri

Million Dollar Belt Match:
Million Dollar Man Ted DiBiase (Champion)
vs. Jake "The Snake" Roberts

Rowdy Roddy Piper vs. Bad News Brown

Big Boss Man vs. Akeem (managed by Slick)

The Rockers vs. Orient Express

Hercules vs. Earthquake

Brutus "The Barber" Beefcake
vs. Mr. Perfect

Hart Foundation vs. The Bolsheviks

Hacksaw Jim Duggan
vs. Dino Bravo (managed by Jimmy Hart)

Superfly Jimmy Snuka vs. Ravishing Rick Rude

Tito Santana vs. The Barbarian

Koko B. Ware vs. The Model Rick Martel

At the dawn of a new decade, the World Wrestling Federation found itself facing a pleasant problem: how to satisfy its mushrooming audience, which now extended well beyond the boundaries of the United States. We were, by this time, extremely popular in Canada, so as discussion about potential sites for *WrestleMania VI* intensified, Toronto's SkyDome became a legitimate option. There was no longer any doubt that we had enough fans and a sufficient marketing machine to meet the task of filling the SkyDome. But that didn't mean the promotion was without its challenges.

First and foremost was the main event between Hulk Hogan and the Ultimate Warrior. When I first heard that this would be the centerpiece of *WrestleMania VI*, I was unabashedly enthusiastic, which just goes to show that even after five years with the company I still had a lot to learn about this business of sports-entertainment. In wrestling parlance, this was a "babyface match." It was two good guys, both of whom were extremely popular. While this type of

OPPOSITE: Hogan traps the Warrior in a modified sleeper hold.

6

Toronto SkyDome
Toronto, Ontario, Canada
April 1, 1990
Attendance: 67,678

match could be aesthetically pleasing, it typically did not sell a lot of tickets. From the fans' standpoint, it was almost like a political race in which both candidates are stressing the issues, and how they're going to make the world a better place, rather than attacking each other. This type of race is entirely proper and, perhaps, more enlightening for the public. For some reason, though, it tends to put people to sleep; voter turnout invariably is low.

It wasn't a great leap to think a similar response might greet *WrestleMania VI*. Here we had Hulk Hogan, the reigning champion, and the Ultimate Warrior, whose style and athleticism appealed to newer fans who were attracted to the glitz and energy of this new star. For six years Hulk had been at the top of the company roster, redefining what it meant to be a superstar in professional wrestling. Six years of Hulkamania; six years of "train, say your prayers, eat your vitamins." Although Hulk was dabbling in other areas of the entertainment world by then, he remained the biggest star in the Federation. When confronted by an opponent whose skills and persona were markedly different, Hulk could still fill an arena with electricity. And that opponent did not necessarily have to be a heel. Randy Savage was not a heel in the traditional sense, but he had his own personality and manner of doing things. The Ultimate Warrior . . . ? He was a good guy. Flamboyant, thickly muscled, attractive. In other words, perhaps a bit too much like Hulk. Whether we could effectively sell this match as a main event in Toronto and maintain the high standards established by previous *WrestleMania*s was cause for legitimate concern.

BELOW: The gladiators sign their contracts for the big event.

OPPOSITE: The Ultimate Warrior became the first challenger to cleanly defeat the Hulkster.

An Awesome Venue The Toronto SkyDome is one of the most unique facilities in North America. It was built primarily as a home for the Toronto Blue Jays baseball team and the Toronto Argonauts of the Canadian Football League, but really it is much more than just an athletic facility. When I went up to visit with SkyDome officials, I discovered there were eighteen different operating companies within this building, including not only the Blue Jays and Argonauts, but also the SkyDome Authority, two different sets of concessions (one for the general public, another for private meetings and functions), a Hard Rock Cafe, and an audiovisual company.

In each of the previous two years, *WrestleMania* had been held in an older, more intimate setting, so there were no giant television screens. The focus was entirely on the ring itself. Now, however, we were going back to a domed stadium, one which, in fact, was so technologically advanced that the massive roof was actually retractable.

One of the great attractions of SkyDome is its ability to perform in any type of weather. On a cold winter day, the stadium is covered; on a clear summer day, the roof is pulled back. Regardless of the lighting or the climate, fans can watch the action not only on the field, but on SkyDome's massive video screen, which is nearly two stories tall. When *WrestleMania* was held at the Pontiac Silverdome, we had been obliged to install video screens, and of course their performance was dependent on the lighting. In Toronto, we would have no such concerns. There would not be a bad seat in the house.

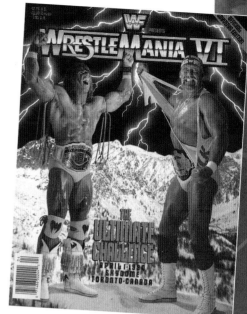

Big News   In working in Toronto, one of the first things we discovered was that Canada had a highly developed professional wrestling business. The World Wrestling Federation had maintained an office in Toronto for many years, and our following throughout Canada had been on the increase for some time. But I'm not sure everyone within the company understood just how deeply ingrained was the passion for wrestling in the Great White North. As an example, consider how *WrestleMania VI* was treated by the mainstream media. Unlike the United States media, newspapers and radio and television stations in Canada were much more willing to suspend disbelief and report on *WrestleMania VI,* both in advance and in review, as pure sport. We didn't promote it this way, of course, but we viewed their zeal and cooperation as a wonderful opportunity. Over the years we had developed a certain way of working with the entertainment sections of newspapers, creating supplement sections, fan guides, that sort of thing. These would always be written in a favorable light, but would basically talk about nothing more than the personalities involved in *WrestleMania,* and not really about the athleticism or the "competition." Which was acceptable, since the World Wrestling Federation was by now quite comfortable in billing itself as "sports-entertainment." In Canada, however, we found ourselves in the unusual position of being covered as a sporting event as well as an entertainment event. In the United States, that hadn't happened in quite some time. Suddenly reporters were strolling into press conferences, notebooks at the ready, and asking such questions as, "How are you going to win?" and "What is your strategy?" It was an amusing development and one that we were more than willing to use as a promotional tool.

Oddly enough, we received a much cooler reception from the various business groups at SkyDome. Some three months before *WrestleMania VI,* we had a memorable and surprising meeting with key representatives from all of these groups—vice presidents, presidents, executive directors. We were all together in a conference room at SkyDome, thanks in part to the efforts of Jack Tunney, who operated as president of WWF Canada. On television, Jack's role was to be no more than a stereotype of what a president would be—it was just a part he was playing. In truth, though, he was our key management person. Jack was well connected and had been around for a long time, so he was able to arrange a meeting with representatives from all of these companies—people who had it within their power to make our job as promoters easier or more difficult. We told them that *WrestleMania VI* was coming to SkyDome and that it would be the biggest event of the year. It would be promoted on two hundred television stations across the United States and twenty stations we worked with in Canada. We assured them we would set the all-time attendance record at SkyDome.

"We want to work with you," we said. "We want to develop sponsorships and co-promotions. We want you to help us make this the best event it can possibly be."

Their response?

"Well . . . we're happy you're here, but . . . "

Not one of those eighteen organizations was willing to work with the World Wrestling Federation. In fact, the Toronto Blue Jays would not even allow us to use their box office or ticketing system. I can honestly say that we have never figured out why they were so uncooperative, but I recall the meeting ending with someone from our company saying, "Thanks for listening to us. We're going to set an attendance record here, with or without your help." And that's precisely what we did. In less than three months we put together this entire promotion and sold 67,678 tickets. We did it absolutely alone—we even had to configure our own box office in the stadium and create our own ticketing system. We grossed more than three million dollars, Canadian. We sold out the SkyDome Hotel. We brought to the city of Toronto one of the most memorable events of the new decade. And we did it despite a complete lack of participation from SkyDome's many operating companies.

Nobody's Fool Since *WrestleMania VI* was being held in Canada, it seemed only appropriate that a Canadian artist be enlisted to sing the national anthem. Robert Goulet accepted the offer. Unfortunately, we found out the day before the event that because he rarely had an opportunity to sing the anthem, Robert might have difficulty remembering all the words to "O Canada," so the lyrics were broadcast on the giant video screen. It all worked out just fine. Interestingly, another celebrity who took part in the event was Steve Allen, who conducted a backstage interview with Nikolai Volkoff—in the men's shower room! Allen, a talk show host, musician, and comedian, has more recently become an outspoken opponent of what critics might call

"objectionable television." Professional wrestling, of course, often falls under that umbrella. But on April Fool's Day 1990, Steve Allen was a willing participant in *WrestleMania VI*, and he actually did a commendable job. I remember there were several riders in his contract regarding the type of room he had, the type of amenities—he was very "Hollywood" in his requirements. But he also was thoroughly engaged and engaging. Steve Allen "got it," and in the end, with him playing the piano, singing, interviewing Nikolai in the shower . . . it was all quite amusing.

Robert Goulet belts out "O Canada."

The Ultimate Challenge You didn't have to be a rocket scientist to figure out where the World Wrestling Federation was headed with *WrestleMania VI*. The main event featured a couple of good guys and was called the "Ultimate Challenge." With Hulk Hogan on top for so long and increasingly vocal about his desire to make movies and otherwise spread his creative wings, it was apparent that the stage was being set for a new champion, for a passing of the torch.

At this time, certainly more than today, the Federation champion shouldered a great deal of individual responsibility. It was true that the championship belt provided considerable income and opportunity for the person who held it, but it was also a heavy burden. The lion's share of revenue for the World Wrestling Federation came from live events, and the success of those events was heavily dependent upon the presence of the champion. Before sports-entertainment became such a dominant presence on television, before the Internet changed the face of marketing, the Federation was much more dependent on selling tickets based on "feuds" and rivalries, most of which centered on the champion. And since the wrestlers earn a percentage of multiple revenue streams, it stands to reason that if there's a sellout, then there's more money for everyone. So the better the champion was, the better it was for the entire company.

There was no doubt that the number of tickets sold in the early days of the *Wrestle-Mania* era was directly proportional to the popularity of the champion. All of the other wrestlers knew this, and so they were supportive of him both in the ring and in other public settings. Behind the scenes, of course, this could foster either respect or resentment, depending on how well the champion did his job. If he worked every day, if he did his job like a pro, the rest of the boys would rally around him. On the other hand, if he insisted on flying only first class and taking days off, if he begged off interviews and stopped going to the gym . . . well, it wasn't long before the rest of team (and it really is a team) started behaving the same way.

Hulk Hogan had carried this responsibility for an exceptionally long period of time. That he might be growing tired of it wasn't a shock to anyone associated with the company. Nevertheless, those of us in the front office didn't really know what was going to happen in the Ultimate Challenge. Strictly from a business standpoint, it didn't matter, because we didn't need to know the outcome in order to do our jobs. So, that night, as I stood in the SkyDome press box watching the main event with my wife, I felt oddly excited. I thought I knew what was going to happen. But I wasn't quite sure. And the fact that the press box was filled with dozens of traditional sports reporters only served to heighten the anxiety and uncertainty. It almost felt like a competitive sports event. A championship *game*.

While I don't think anyone would confuse Hulk or the Ultimate Warrior with Ted DiBiase or Randy Savage or The Rock—some of the really great technical wrestlers—there was an undeniable electricity in the building that night. Hulk was decked out in his usual yellow and red, and the Ultimate Warrior was wearing orange and pink, with streamers flowing from his

WrestleMania VI seemed to grip the entire city of Toronto.

biceps and legs. Together they put on an intensely entertaining match, with a lot of twists and turns. At one point, as both men lay on the mat at the same time, having knocked each other nearly unconscious, the ref stood over them . . . counting.

"*One . . . two . . .* "

To no one in particular, and to my own surprise, I started rooting under my breath. "Come on! Get up!"

My wife looked at me in disbelief. "You're cheering?" she said. "You don't know what's going to happen? Or you do know, and you're rooting anyway? Explain this to me."

I shrugged. "Well, I think I know what's supposed to happen. But I'm not sure."

That was the truth. Maybe in the last twenty-four hours Hulk had changed his mind. God knows that had happened before. Maybe he wanted to work for another year. You know, it could be fun at the top . . . and lucrative, too. It was not at all out of the realm of possibility that something unexpected could happen. And as a matter of fact, Hulk did stage a comeback after seemingly being knocked out. It looked for a few moments as though he was going to retain the championship belt. In the end, though, the Ultimate Warrior turned the tables and pinned Hulk. It was a clean, decisive victory.

Afterward, Hulk handed the belt to the Warrior, hugged him, and gave the thumbs-up sign to the fans, much as he had done for Randy Savage two years earlier. The lasting image I have from *Wrestle-Mania VI* is Hulk Hogan climbing into the little cart that was used to speed the wrestlers to and from the ring. Hulk . . . glistening with sweat, his hair matted, staring off into space as the crowd screamed and applauded. I'm still not sure whether they were cheering for the new champion . . . or saying good-bye to the old one.

OPPOSITE: The ref counts after the brawlers collided in center ring.

BELOW: The titans embrace after the historic title change.

WrestleMania VII

**World Wrestling Federation
Title Match:**
Sergeant Slaughter (Champion—
managed by General Adnan) vs. Hulk Hogan

Career Match:
Ultimate Warrior vs.
Macho King Randy Savage (with Queen Sherri)

**World Wrestling Federation
Tag Team Title Match:**
Hart Foundation (Champions)
vs. The Nasty Boys (managed by Jimmy Hart)

Virgil (with Rowdy Roddy Piper in his corner)
vs. Million Dollar Man Ted DiBiase

**World Wrestling Federation
Intercontinental Title Match:**
Mr. Perfect (Champion—
managed by Bobby "The Brain" Heenan)
vs. Big Boss Man

Blindfold Match:
Jake "The Snake" Roberts vs. The Model Rick Martel

Superfly Jimmy Snuka vs. The Undertaker
(managed by Paul Bearer)

Tito Santana vs. The Mountie (managed by Jimmy Hart)

Greg "The Hammer" Valentine
vs. Earthquake (managed by Slick)

Texas Tornado vs. Dino Bravo (managed by Jimmy Hart)

Tenryu & Kitao vs. Demolition (managed by Mr. Fuji)

British Bulldog vs. Warlord (managed by Slick)

The Rockers vs. The Barbarian & Haku
(managed by Bobby "The Brain" Heenan)

Legion of Doom vs. Power & Glory

WrestleMania VII was interesting right from the start. Originally scheduled to be held at the Los Angeles Coliseum, it was moved to the Coliseum's smaller, indoor neighbor, the Los Angeles Sports Arena, when concerns over security arose in the wake of the Persian Gulf War. Current events have always tended to shape the business of professional wrestling in general, and *WrestleMania* in particular. But this was one time when current events really conspired against the promotion and actually dictated that changes be made.

By the end of 1990 mounting tension between the United States and Iraq caused the United States to begin sending greater numbers of troops to the Middle East. Anger over Iraq's conflict with its neighbor Kuwait escalated and there was a natural stoking of ill will toward the Iraqi government among American citizens, much as there had been toward the Soviet Union during the height of the Cold War. To tap into this emotional wellspring, the World Wrestling Federation created a scenario in which Hulk Hogan, the unabashed patriot, the "Real American," would engage in a heated rivalry with an Iraqi sympathizer, with the climax coming at *WrestleMania VII*. The great irony of this plot was the character chosen for the role of heel: Sergeant Slaughter.

Sarge, of course, was the embodiment of patriotism before Hulk came along. He dressed in military regalia and proudly displayed his love for the U.S. flag. In 1991, however, Sergeant Slaughter was

BELOW: The theme of *WrestleMania VII* was the Persian Gulf War.
OPPOSITE: The Ultimate Warrior's hand is raised after his match with Randy Savage.

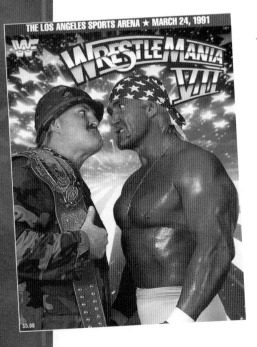

7

Los Angeles Sports Arena
Los Angeles, California
March 24, 1991
Attendance: 16,158

no longer a member of the Federation roster. And since he had been a babyface headliner in his own right, when Sarge came back, he had to come back in a way that would make it interesting for the fans. The result: Sergeant Slaughter would become a traitor, as well as the new champion. It proved to be one of the most fascinating turns in Federation history, and the resulting story line evoked passionate responses from fans throughout the country.

After Sarge was pictured on the cover of *WWF Magazine* with a character named General Adnan, who bore a striking resemblance to Iraq's hated leader Saddam Hussein, he began receiving threats on his life. When he went out in public—even if he wasn't in character—people would taunt him. He was refused service in restaurants. Rarely had a story line so strongly gripped the public. It was great theater, great storytelling, and the perfect promotional hook for making Hulk, who had returned to the fold after taking time off to make a movie, the savior of the flag yet again.

ABOVE: Sergeant Slaughter portrayed a Marine turned Iraqi sympathizer.

OPPOSITE: Patriotism ruled the Los Angeles Sports Arena.

Reality and Fantasy Collide

The company's enthusiasm for this promotion waned in late January, when war broke out and the United States began bombing Iraq. American servicemen were being killed overseas, and suddenly a well-placed, smart promotion seemed to be bordering on bad taste. But we were stuck with it.

Promoting any major event was problematic during this period—at the Super Bowl in Tampa, Florida, for example, threats of terrorism prompted a dramatic increase in security, including metal detectors at every gate. In this highly emotional atmosphere, the World Wrestling Federation was planning an outdoor event at the Los Angeles Coliseum, with an anticipated crowd of approximately 90,000 and a main event featuring an Iraqi sympathizer. This certainly did not sound like a great idea. So, after the Super Bowl, in late January a meeting was held and a decision was made to change the venue.

This was no small matter. We were well into the marketing process by this point. We had been to Los Angeles several times. We had created a seating chart and completed a site survey. Tickets had been on sale for nearly a month. In fact, we had already sold 16,000 seats. We were fortunate that the Los Angeles Sports Arena is located right next door to the Coliseum, which simplified the move somewhat. Nevertheless, the sudden shift created several problems, the most obvious of which was the fact that we had to immediately stop selling tickets because the event was virtually sold out. It was at once a marketing godsend and a nightmare. Certainly it was a much better situation—not having to promote this main event for ticket sales, especially in light of the war casualties. On the other hand, we

had sold these tickets based on an outdoor venue with a much different seating configuration. At the Coliseum there were forty seats in the front row of each side of the ring; at the Sports Arena there were twenty seats in the front row.

When someone buys a front-row seat, of course, they expect a front-row seat. But at *WrestleMania VII*, there were twice as many front-row ticket holders as there were front-row seats. So that became the number one marketing task for the next eight weeks: working with the arena, sending out letters to ticket holders, advertising in every possible medium—doing everything we possibly could to reach out to our fans and exchange the tickets. By March 30, the day before *WrestleMania VII*, we had exchanged 11,000 tickets.

LEFT TO RIGHT: The stars come out in Hollywood: Willie Nelson sings "America the Beautiful"; Alex Trebek, Marla Maples, and Regis Philbin greet the crowd; Chuck Norris observes the action; Henry "The Fonz" Winkler lost in thought; Macauley Culkin hangs out at ringside.

That meant we would still have to exchange 5,000 at the gate on the day of the event. This involved a tremendous organizational effort, including setting up temporary ticket windows outside the venue. *WrestleMania VII* was scheduled to begin at 4:00 P.M. Pacific time. At 3:30, just thirty minutes before the first match, there were still several thousand people outside the Sports Arena, waiting in line to exchange their tickets. Making matters even worse, the computers went down minutes before the event was to begin, and we still had people stuck outside. Believe me, there was a lot of tension around the Los Angeles Sports Arena that day.

The Stars Come Out Thankfully, once all ticket holders were inside, the event went smoothly. Since *WrestleMania VII* was held in Los Angeles, it was only fitting that it attracted a star-studded crowd. In addition to the celebrities who were invited to participate in the event—Donald Trump's new companion, Marla Maples, was timekeeper, Willie Nelson sang "America the Beautiful," and Regis Philbin and Alex Trebek were guest announcers—*WrestleMania VII* featured an interesting trio of Hollywood tough guys, none of whom was being paid to appear. The first was Chuck Norris, star of a string of action-adventure movies. The second was Lou Ferrigno, who for several years had starred in the popular television series *The Incredible Hulk*. It was interesting—Lou was

there with his kids, and he said that their favorite wrestler was Hulk Hogan. As they stood
behind Lou screaming, "Hulk! Hulk! Hulk!" Lou smiled.

"It's weird to hear them say that when they're not talking about me," he said.

The third "tough guy" was Henry Winkler, who played the legendary "Fonz" on
Happy Days. Henry was there with some kids and clearly was attending the show for their
benefit. We asked him for an interview and he graciously agreed. Henry got right into the
spirit of the whole thing—there was no air of superiority or anything like that. He was a
real gentleman. During the intermission (this was the last *WrestleMania,* incidentally, to
have an intermission), we invited Henry and his kids to join us in a private area where we
had refreshments, just to be away from the crowd for a few minutes. Then, immediately
following the event, we offered them an opportunity to slide out a back door. But Henry
declined. He said he didn't see any need for that, and he and his group left with the rest of
the crowd. About a week later I received a handwritten note from Henry thanking me for
treating him and his family so well. I have always thought he was a great example of class.

Together Again   *WrestleMania VII* included one of the more interesting
undercard matches in the history of the event: Randy Savage vs. the Ultimate Warrior.
What made it special was not so much the action in the ring—although both men are
highly athletic and did in fact put on a great show—but the surprise resolution of a story
line that had captivated fans for months.

Randy and his manager, Miss Elizabeth, had been estranged, so when Randy entered the ring for his battle with the Ultimate Warrior, he did so with a voluptuous new manager, the Sensational Queen Sherri, on his arm. What Randy's character did not know was that Miss Elizabeth was in the stands that night. I had escorted Liz to a seat in the third or fourth row. The plan was for her to watch the match and become increasingly distraught as Randy took a beating at the hands of the Ultimate Warrior. When she could finally take it no longer, Miss Elizabeth would jump out of her seat, run down the aisle, swing over the barricades, and leap into the ring. The camera would capture not only the in-ring action, but Miss Elizabeth's pained reactions. The crowd quickly realized there was a star in their midst and kept rushing over to Liz and asking for her autograph. Throughout the match we were concerned that each time the camera cut to Miss Elizabeth, viewers would be treated to a shot of a celebrity mingling with her fans, rather than what was supposed to be a candid glimpse of a woman aching for the man she once loved . . . and probably still did love. The World Wrestling Federation isn't averse to breaking down the fourth wall once in a while, but it's hard to suspend disbelief when the characters are chatting with fans. It was a harrowing twenty minutes, not only in the ring, but in the crowd as well.

As it happened, the production came off cleanly. Randy lost the match to the Ultimate Warrior, and as he lay on the mat, broken and barely conscious, his manager turned on him. Queen Sherri, angry that her meal ticket had been beaten (worse, really, since this was a "loser must retire" match), began kicking and berating Randy, humiliating him in front of a worldwide audience. As this was happening, Miss Elizabeth charged into the ring, grabbed Sherri, and tossed her over the ropes. Then, as the crowd went wild, she rushed to the side of her former lover. It was among the best *WrestleMania* moments I've seen— Randy Savage, whose moniker is the Macho Man, looking up and seeing Liz, realizing that she had come to his rescue. They fell into an embrace, held it, and then walked out of the ring together . . . a team once again.

TOP: The Macho King with Queen Sherri.
LEFT: The Warrior reaches out and touches Savage.
OPPOSITE: Savage and Miss Elizabeth are finally reunited.

But there was an immediate and obvious change in the parameters of their relationship. For years it had been the Macho Man's style to force Miss Elizabeth to wait on him hand and foot. When he entered the ring, she held the ropes apart for him. Now, though, as Randy leaned through the ropes, with Liz in her usual position, Randy suddenly stopped. He sat down on the second rope, lifted the top rope, and graciously, in a gentlemanly way, ushered Miss Elizabeth through ahead of him. The ensuing roar was as loud as anything I had ever heard at *WrestleMania,* and I swear there were people actually crying in the stands. Of course, none of it was spontaneous. This was the way it was planned, which to me was the most amazing thing of all—that there was a clear understanding of what the crowd really wanted to see. With one simple gesture, Randy's character came full circle, and the crowd was treated to precisely the payoff it expected and deserved.

The main event between Hulk Hogan and Sergeant Slaughter was an entertaining match, although perhaps not quite as unique and dramatic as the Randy Savage–Ultimate Warrior encounter. With General Adnan (his commanding officer) in his corner, Sergeant Slaughter utilized all manner of dirty tricks to gain the upper hand and further enrage the crowd. Sarge even spit in the face of the Real American when Hulk was down, and proceeded to drape the Iraqi flag over his victim. This, of course, not only provoked howls of protestation from the crowd, but it had a strangely invigorating effect on Hulk. Enraged, he jumped to his feet, took control of the match, and recaptured the championship.

Even in victory, though, the character of Hulk Hogan had taken another step away from invincibility. He left the ring wearing a mask of blood, symbolic of the fact that while Hulk Hogan was still capable of wearing the belt, he was no longer the unscathed superhero who had dominated sports-entertainment through the 1980s. This was Hulk Hogan, not John Wayne.

LEFT: Slaughter punishes Hogan with the camel clutch.
ABOVE: The Hulkster celebrates his win with the red, white, and blue.

WRESTLEMANIA VIII

**World Wrestling Federation
Title Match:**
 Ric Flair (Champion—
 with Executive Consultant Mr. Perfect)
 vs. Macho Man Randy Savage

Second Main Event Match:
 Hulk Hogan vs. Sid Justice

**World Wrestling Federation
Intercontinental Title
Match:**
 Rowdy Roddy Piper (Champion)
 vs. Bret "Hit Man" Hart

**World Wrestling
Federation Tag Team
Title Match:**
 Money, Inc.
 (Champions—managed by Jimmy Hart)
 vs. The Natural Disasters
 (Earthquake & Typhoon)

 The Undertaker (managed by Paul Bearer)
 vs. Jake "The Snake" Roberts

**Eight-Man
Tag Team Match:**
 Sergeant Slaughter, Big Boss Man,
 Hacksaw Jim Duggan & Virgil
 vs. The Nasty Boys, The Mountie & Repo Man

 El Matador vs. Shawn Michaels
 (managed by Sensational Sherri)

 Tatanka vs. The Model Rick Martel

 The Rocket Owen Hart vs. Skinner

WrestleMania VIII represented something of a homecoming for me. I had been involved in the first event ever held in the Hoosier Dome, an exhibition basketball game between the United States Olympic team and a group of NBA All-Stars in the summer of 1984. The Olympic team was coached by Indiana University's Bob Knight, and as a producer of Knight's weekly television show in Indianapolis, I had the opportunity to arrange the broadcast of this game. As it turned out, that event drew 67,000 fans, which was then the largest crowd ever to see a basketball game. *WrestleMania VIII,* nearly eight years later, would come close to equaling that figure, but it would prove to be a more challenging promotion.

As was the case in Toronto in 1990, this version of *WrestleMania* featured an intriguing twist, but one that was not guaranteed to be successful. *WrestleMania VI* had culminated in a babyface main event between Hulk Hogan and the Ultimate Warrior. The

OPPOSITE: Randy Savage tugs at Ric Flair's flaxen locks during their championship match.

hook this time was a double main event: Randy Savage against champion Ric Flair in one match, and Hulk Hogan against Sid Justice in the other. At first glance this might seem like a great idea—*two sensational matches for the price of one!* From a marketing standpoint, though, it really wasn't that simple. Whenever a card (and this holds true for boxing, as well) features more than one main event, there is always the risk of diffusing the focus and excitement. So the challenge for us was to make sure that our

8

Hoosier Dome
Indianapolis, Indiana
April 5, 1992
Attendance: 62,167

fans understood why *WrestleMania VIII* would be a great event and what was unique about each match. Since the event was being held in a domed stadium, this was especially true. If the promotion didn't work, there was a chance we'd have a bunch of empty seats—and that had never happened at *WrestleMania*.

The first major event of the marketing campaign was a press conference at the Indianapolis Convention Center, adjacent to the Hoosier Dome, and it was one of the few times I can recall the staff actually surprising Vince McMahon. Typically, Vince was deeply involved in every piece of the marketing plan, but he was a little in the dark on this particular press event.

In addition to several of the participants in *WrestleMania VIII*, the press conference included a number of local dignitaries and more than a hundred media representatives. It was held in one of the big convention halls, and the "room" was bisected by a floor-to-ceiling curtain; the dais was in front of the curtain. Everyone was introduced and said a few words, and we went through the normal trappings of a press conference. Near the end, Hulk Hogan was introduced. Hulk was not

TOP: Hogan barreled into a press conference on this customized bus.

ABOVE: Hogan bonds with some young Hulkamaniacs in Indianapolis.

on the dais at the time. Instead, he came barreling through the curtain in a Hulkamania bus. (Actually, it was an Indianapolis Metro bus that had been decorated with Hulk's image, the word "Hulkamania," and information about *WrestleMania*.) The bus drove straight through the curtain and into the press conference, in the process knocking the breath out of everyone in attendance. When the bus came to a halt, Hulk stepped out—followed by sixty little kids wearing Hulkamania bandannas and waving American flags.

To say it was a dramatic entrance would be one hell of an understatement, and everyone seemed to love it. What we didn't know was whether or not Vince would approve. In the end, those who worked on this plan were really gratified. As the kids poured out of the bus behind Hulk like a scene straight out of *Rocky,* with "Real American" playing over the sound system, Vince smiled and congratulated the staff. We don't take chances like that too often, and it was rewarding to have it work out so well.

Straight from the Heartland

WrestleMania VIII had a decidedly Middle America flavor, which was appropriate for Indianapolis. Country music star Reba McEntire sang a gorgeous a capella version of "America the Beautiful." Ray Combs, host of the television game show *Family Feud,* was the ring announcer. Having lived in Indianapolis and worked with the Indiana Pacers, I had developed some good professional relationships with people in the city, which was helpful when we began promoting *WrestleMania VIII.* But we quickly discovered that when it came to the World Wrestling Federation and *WrestleMania,* some significant misconceptions remained.

Indianapolis prides itself on being the amateur sports capital of the world. And rightly so. The city has hosted the National Sports Festival, the Pan Am Games, the NCAA Final Four, and numerous other events. It also serves as headquarters to a variety of amateur athletic organizations. Additionally, Indianapolis has the Pacers and the NFL's Colts. So, even though it's a relatively small city, it really is something of a sports Mecca.

In 1992 a friend of mine was running the Indiana Sports Corporation, a not-for-profit organization dedicated to promoting amateur sports, and to furthering Indianapolis's reputation as the amateur sports capital. In trying to figure out the most efficient and respectful way to work with the city, we decided to approach the Sports Corporation with a proposal. We offered them a donation of one dollar for every ticket sold in exchange for their endorsement. We wanted to be able to put a tag line in the local newspaper ads, and we wanted to do a mailing offering their tens of thousands of members a preferred ticket opportunity or something of that nature. I told my friend, who was the executive director of the organization, that we would be selling between 62,000 and 64,000 seats (the final count was 62,167)—there was no question about that. We'd sell as many seats as we could put in there, with or without the help of their organization. But we thought offering them an endorsement opportunity was the right thing to do. A few weeks later she called me back to say the board of directors had turned down the invitation. I was surprised. They had simply walked away from a significant donation to amateur sports in their city, apparently because they did not want to be associated with professional wrestling. To this day I take every opportunity to give my friend a hard time about how her organization turned down the easiest money they could ever have made.

Hulk's Farewell?

The buildup to *WrestleMania VIII* focused heavily on the possibility that fans were about to see the final performance of Hulk Hogan. Vince McMahon, who was still portraying the character of an on-camera

81

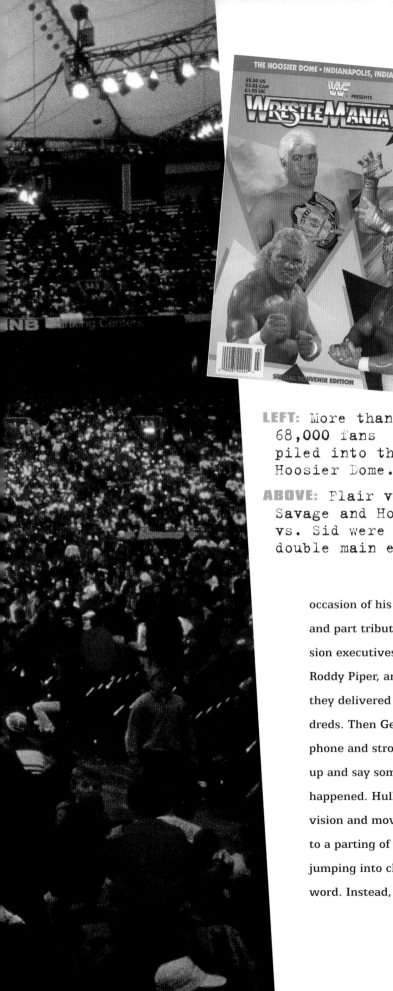

THE HOOSIER DOME • INDIANAPOLIS, INDIANA • APRIL 5, 1992

$3.50 US
$3.95 CAN
£1.95 UK

WWF PRESENTS

WrestleMania VIII

SPECIAL SOUVENIR EDITION

WWF

LEFT: More than 68,000 fans piled into the Hoosier Dome.

ABOVE: Flair vs. Savage and Hogan vs. Sid were the double main events.

announcer and reporter, hosted a particularly memorable interview with Hulk just a few weeks prior to the event. It was conducted on a dark, sparse set, with Hulk wearing a black, oversize sweatshirt rather than one of his usual yellow-and-red outfits. The look was very stark, and Hulk's demeanor was calm, serious, reflecting a quiet resolve. They discussed the match and the possibility that it would be Hulk's finale, even though it was not a title match. For years Hulk had been walking that fine line between staying in the business and leaving, and he continued to do that now. What really struck me about the interview, though, was that they talked about what Hulk had meant to professional wrestling.

At the end of the interview Vince McMahon, still in character, turned to Hulk Hogan and said, "Thank you for what you've brought to the World Wrestling Federation and your fans worldwide." Hulk nodded and shook Vince's hand.

It was extremely well done, and like all the best spots in sports-entertainment, very close to the edge of real emotion. It also stood in dramatic contrast to another, earlier event featuring both Vince and Hulk, a surprise party at the Rainbow Room in New York in 1991, given for Vince on the occasion of his twenty-fifth anniversary in the business of professional wrestling. Part roast and part tribute, the evening featured videotaped presentations from celebrities and television executives, as well as speeches from many of those in attendance. Randy Savage, Roddy Piper, and several other wrestlers went to great lengths to prepare remarks, and they delivered them with the appropriate blend of humor and emotion to a crowd of hundreds. Then Gene Okerlund, at the time a very popular broadcaster, took a wireless microphone and strolled casually around the room, giving other people an opportunity to stand up and say something about Vince. When Gene got to Hulk Hogan, an extraordinary thing happened. Hulk, who could perform in front of tens of thousands of people, who was a television and movie star, suddenly was at a loss for words. He and Vince obviously had come to a parting of the ways, but it had not yet happened. Instead of taking the microphone and jumping into character, or saying something in the spirit of the event, Hulk didn't say a word. Instead, he waved Okerlund off.

It was an embarrassing moment, and I remember thinking, *What's going on?* This was a guy I'd seen in airports, in arenas, in business settings, in stadiums . . . wherever he was, he always rose to the occasion. Whatever else he was, Hulk Hogan was a true performer. I was shocked by his behavior in this setting, because he was a man who could bring a crowd of 50,000 to its feet merely by twisting his hand and putting it behind his ear, as if listening for a cheer. He could have done anything—*anything!*—and it would have been enough to satisfy this room. But instead, Hulk did nothing. Remembering the way Hulk had acted that night in the Rainbow Room, I was particularly struck now by his interview with Vince. True, it was part of the promotion for Vince to shake Hulk's hand and say thank you, but it seemed that there really was some heartfelt emotion behind the words. I have always been disappointed that Hulk wasn't as gracious.

Three Memorable Matches

Although *WrestleMania VIII* was billed as a double main event, it actually featured a third compelling confrontation, between Bret Hart and Roddy Piper. Bret had long been highly regarded for his wrestling ability, and Roddy was a pretty respectable athlete in his own right, as well as a legitimate boxer and all-around tough guy. Roddy, who occasionally put on a little excess weight, had gotten into great shape for this match, and he and Bret put on a phenomenal show, a very physical, athletic performance. Moreover, it was an interesting story line that surrounded their battle. This was a grudge match between two friends and rivals, with the Intercontinental title on the line. The highlight of the match came when Roddy, clearly in control, grabbed the ring bell, which was mounted on a piece of solid wood, and prepared to smack his fallen opponent in the face. But he couldn't bring himself to deliver the blow. That moment of weakness, which worked beautifully because it was so antithetical to the nature of "Rowdy" Roddy Piper, proved to be a fatal mistake. Bret had time to recover and ultimately came back to win the match.

Afterward, in a rare display of camaraderie, Roddy placed the belt on Bret. Then they did something I had never before seen two wrestlers do (and, in fact, have never seen since): they left the ring arm in arm. Such behavior was always believed to be too corny, something the fans would not accept. But in this context, it worked.

The match between Ric Flair and Randy Savage was another example of reality and fantasy intersecting in such a way that the event cut closer to the bone. Ric had been making public comments about Miss Elizabeth, Randy Savage's manager (and now his wife), insinuating that Liz was secretly attracted to the "Nature Boy." This, obviously, enraged Randy, which of course is precisely the effect it would have had on him in real life. Ric was great at this sort of promotion. He had perfected a loud, brash persona and was brilliant at turning in over-the-top bad-guy performances. Not a bad guy in the sense of being a froth-

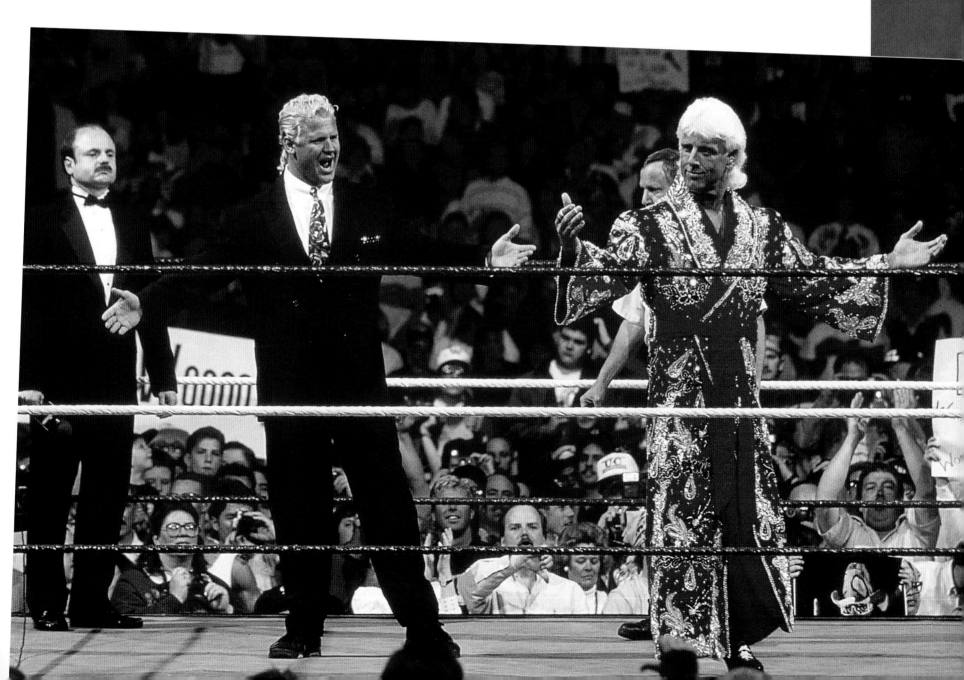

ing, uncontrollable maniac; rather, a bad guy who dressed well, who was articulate, who had thick blond hair, and who was in general a striking character. He also happened to be a technically proficient wrestler from the old school, in which matches were physical and it was assumed you'd take a beating once in a while. Ric was kind of fair-skinned, and he was willing to take a lot of backhand slaps across the chest early in his matches, because the effect was truly dramatic. You could see the welts rising on his skin, and you knew they had to sting like mad, but Ric would keep taunting his opponent, daring him to hit even harder. And the sound of each slap—skin on skin—would echo through the building.

In some areas of the country Ric's popularity rivaled that of Hulk Hogan's. He could wrestle, he could work the mike, and he knew the business. Although he lost the championship belt to an impassioned Randy Savage, Ric's performance was one of the highlights of *Wrestle-Mania VIII,* and represented perhaps the high point of his World Wrestling Federation career.

Such was not the case with Hulk Hogan, whose aura of invincibility was further eroded during his match with Sid Justice. Triple-teamed by Justice, Papa Shango, and Justice's manager, Dr. Harvey Wippleman, Hulk was on the verge of an embarrassing defeat when he was joined by the Ultimate Warrior, whose entrance—a fifty-yard dash with colors flying and his costume flowing behind him—provoked the loudest ovation of the night. It was, in fact, one of the more amazing entrances ever seen, so dramatic that it actually overshadowed what happened in the ring afterward. Hulk ultimately triumphed, and in the end he stood alongside the Warrior, soaking up the cheers of the crowd. In a sense, though, it was not his victory. Rather than winning, he had been rescued, and that was a new experience for Hulk Hogan.

LEFT: The Macho Man sends the Nature Boy tumbling over the ropes.

TOP RIGHT: Sid Justice works over the Hulkster with a nerve hold.

RIGHT: The night climaxed with the Ultimate Warrior rushing to Hogan's rescue.

WrestleMania IX

World Wrestling Federation Title Match:
Bret "Hit Man" Hart (Champion)
vs. Yokozuna (managed by Mr. Fuji)

World Wrestling Federation Tag Team Title Match:
Money, Inc. (Million Dollar Man Ted DiBiase
& IRS—Champions)
vs. Mega-Maniacs (Hulk Hogan
& Brutus "The Barber" Beefcake
—managed by Jimmy Hart)

World Wrestling Federation Intercontinental Title Match:
Shawn Michaels (Champion—with Luna Vachon)
vs. Tatanka (with Sensational Sherri)

The Undertaker (managed by Paul Bearer)
vs. Giant Gonzalez (managed by Harvey Wippleman)

Crush vs. Doink the Clown

Mr. Perfect vs. The Narcissist Lex Luger

Tag Team Match:
Steiner Brothers vs. Head Shrinkers (managed by Afa)

Bob Backlund vs. Razor Ramon

By the end of 1992, as we began making plans for *WrestleMania IX,* it had become clear that Hulk Hogan was no longer actively involved with the World Wrestling Federation. For several years his presence had been inconsistent. He'd been in and out . . . in and out. Now, though, it looked as though he had definitely decided to pursue other business and entertainment interests, and there were no plans for him to be part of *WrestleMania IX.* Exactly what the main event would be was uncertain. Hulk had cast a long shadow, and his apparent exit made this a transitional period for the Federation in general and for *WrestleMania* in particular.

Eventually it was decided that Bret Hart, the Federation champion, would face the mammoth Yokozuna, a mysterious character who supposedly had been a championship-caliber sumo wrestler. While this was an interesting and unusual match, it was not the most obvious promotion imaginable. After all, it's not like sumo wrestling is a big attraction in the United States. Although Yokozuna was, for his size, a highly athletic and acrobatic man, and Bret was one of the most technically sound performers in the company, this was not the type of match that would sell 70,000 or 80,000 tickets. It was a complicated and challenging event to market.

As it happened, we didn't have to sell that many tickets, since *WrestleMania IX* was held at Caesars Palace in Las Vegas, in a 16,000-seat outdoor stadium. There were concerns

BELOW: Hulk Hogan was in the promotional back row, behind Hart and Yokozuna.

OPPOSITE: The Hit Man mounts the turnbuckles and pummels Yokozuna.

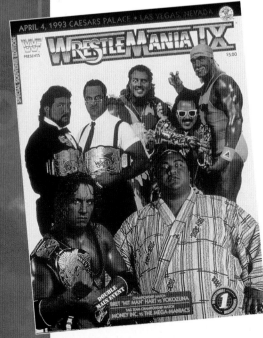

about this, of course. Caesars had hosted literally hundreds of events over the years, including some of the biggest and most memorable championship boxing matches in history, and the weather had almost always cooperated. Still, it was an outdoor venue, and even in Las Vegas it can rain. To address this worry, and to ensure that at least the participants would be kept dry, we constructed a temporary roof over the ring. More problematic was the fact that *WrestleMania IX* would be held almost entirely in daylight in what really was nothing more than a glorified tennis facility, with wooden bleachers on three sides. Virtually all of the great boxing matches had been held at night, when the clear Nevada sky could do wonders for the appearance of the facility and the atmosphere of the event. *WrestleMania IX* would have to stand on its own, and there was legitimate concern that the site would be aesthetically unappealing.

Caesars Palace, however, had made such an attractive offer that the risk was deemed worthwhile. Caesars had guaranteed that our revenue from the event would exceed the revenue of *WrestleMania VIII,* despite the fact that we were very careful to point out to Caesars officials that Hulk Hogan would not be part of the promotion. Their optimism, I think, stemmed at least partly from a reluctance to believe we were telling the truth. One of the Caesars executives was a friend of mine; he was also a knowledgeable wrestling fan, and after we described our marketing plan, which did not include Hulk, he just smiled.

"Yeah, sure. Whatever you say. But I know he'll be there."

"No, he won't be there," I said. "And it's important you understand that Hulk is not part of this event. He is *not* coming back."

My friend nodded slyly, as if in on some sort of secret. "Okay, you guys do what you have to do. We're totally confident, and whether Hulk is there or not, everything will be fine." He paused, smiled again. "But we know he'll be there."

There was no convincing him or anyone else at Caesars Palace that Hulk really had parted ways with the World Wrestling Federation. This was not just part of the event. When we signed our contract with Caesars Palace, we did so fully intending to create a Hulk-less *WrestleMania.* That it didn't turn out that way was purely coincidental.

The World's Biggest Toga Party For

the first and only time in *WrestleMania* history, we went with a specific

TOP: Manager Mr. Fuji stands between his charge Yokozuna and Hart.

ABOVE: *WrestleMania IX* was the toast of the gambling mecca of Las Vegas.

OPPOSITE: Caesar's cup runneth over with World Wrestling Federation devotees.

OPPOSITE, RIGHT: Announcer Jim Ross looked fetching in his toga.

and complete motif. Hundreds of thousands of dollars were spent in an effort to transform a rather mundane tennis stadium into a replica of the Roman Colosseum. The announcers for the event, Jim Ross and Gorilla Monsoon, were dressed in togas. Todd Pettengill, a New York radio personality who had just joined us as a broadcaster and roving reporter, roamed through the stands wearing a baseball cap and toga. Historical characters commonly associated with Rome, such as Caesar and Cleopatra, made grand entrances, as did many of the Federation superstars. Bobby Heenan, for example, rode in on an elephant! From start to finish, the Roman theme was maintained, helping this version of *WrestleMania*, perhaps more than any other, take on the image of a passion play.

To their credit, the people at Caesars Palace really got into the spirit of the event. As with the Emmy Awards and the Oscars, a betting line was made on some of the matches at *WrestleMania.* Even though the line was marked "for entertainment purposes only," some people were more than willing to try to put down a bet. I remember walking into the Caesars Palace sports book and making a wager on a basketball game. On the way back from the window, I spotted another of our employees, a guy who had something of a propensity for making a friendly wager. As I approached, I slowed down, and very seriously, quietly, without breaking stride, I leaned over and said, "They just let me get a bet down on Bret." I had a good laugh as the poor guy nearly tore a hamstring running to the window. Obviously, he never made the bet, and as it turned out it wouldn't have been a smart move, anyway. But that would be the ultimate gift for someone in the wrestling business: to have an opportunity to place a legal bet on the outcome of a match.

Hulkamania . . . One Last Time

Through some eleventh-hour wheeling and dealing, Hulk Hogan was added to the card at *WrestleMania IX*—but not as a headliner. Instead, he was paired with Brutus Beefcake in a tag team championship match against Ted DiBiase and Mike Rotundo, a duo known as Money, Inc. When the folks at Caesars found out about this, they became convinced that we had been sandbagging, that it had always been part of the plan for Hulk to participate in *WrestleMania IX.* Not only that, but my executive friend at Caesars was quite vocal in stating his belief that there was no way the World Wrestling Federation was going to leave Caesars Palace, and this wonderful setting, in this historic spot, without Hulk Hogan as the champion. I told him that he was crazy, that Hulk wasn't even in the championship match, and that even his tag team appearance had been unforeseen. But he wasn't buying it.

LEFT: Hogan and Brutus Beefcake with manager Jimmy Hart.

RIGHT: The weather held up at the first outdoor *WrestleMania.*

In truth, after the previous six months, during which we had heard some wild speculation regarding Hulk's role within the company, there was more than a little tension surrounding his participation in *WrestleMania IX*. When Hulk, atypically, arrived in Las Vegas a day later than scheduled for the event, it didn't bode well. On the eve of *WrestleMania IX* he was supposed to appear at a VIP party. He arrived late, wearing sunglasses and his trademark bandanna, and did a very cursory walk-through. While Brutus Beefcake and Jimmy Hart, the manager of the Mega-Maniacs (as Hulk and Brutus were billed), stayed and posed for pictures and did an admirable amount of schmoozing, Hulk simply left. This was not the way Hulk usually operated. He was a master at working a room.

Clearly, something was wrong.

The next morning, around nine o'clock, I was summoned to Vince McMahon's room. When I got there, Vince was sitting at a table, drinking coffee with his wife, Linda. They seemed quiet, concerned.

"We have a problem," Vince said.

"What?"

"Hulk has had an accident."

Apparently, Hulk had taken a pretty good fall while riding a jet ski during a trip to the beach a few days earlier. When he landed, the left side of his face had taken the brunt of the blow, and now it looked as though he had broken his eye socket. His entire cheek was swollen and hard, and his eye was badly discolored. Not just the area around his eye, but the eyeball itself. All of this, of course, helped explain his behavior the previous night. It also raised some serious questions about *WrestleMania IX*.

"I don't know if Hulk will be able to go today," Vince said. "What do we have to do if he has to come out of the event?"

The answer was at once simple and complicated. We would do the right thing, as always. During much of the planning phase of *WrestleMania IX*, it was assumed that Hulk would not be participating. The fact that he was a late addition who was appearing only in a tag team match, and not the headliner, lessened the severity of the sit-

BELOW: Beefcake holds "Million Dollar Man" DiBiase for a "sledgehammer" from Hogan.

OPPOSITE: The Hulkster unloads on both members of Money, Inc.

uation. Still, Hulk was a marquee name—probably the biggest star in the history of professional wrestling—and his withdrawal was bound to anger and disappoint some fans. We would immediately have to make announcements to the Pay-Per-View audience that Hulk might not be available, and that would no doubt lead not only to a shrinking of the Pay-Per-View audience, but probably a lot of refunding as well. But we had no choice. The fact was, as of that morning, we weren't sure whether Hulk was capable of performing, and if he was capable, we had to make sure that he wouldn't be taking an unreasonable risk and that his performance would be up to his standards.

So, from nine o'clock that morning until the middle of the afternoon, I did not know whether Hulk would be taking part in *WrestleMania IX*. In the interest of fairness and full disclosure, I told some of the Caesars Palace executive staff what was happening, that in fact Hulk Hogan had sustained an injury and might not be able to participate in *Wrestle-Mania IX*. While they accepted this news graciously, they clearly believed I was giving them inaccurate information. They were convinced this was just the latest chapter in the *Wrestle-Mania* saga. To them, the line between reality and fiction had become hopelessly blurred.

Expect the Unexpected
Wearing a bandage over his left eye (to protect the stitches he had taken), Hulk Hogan appeared as scheduled in the tag team championship match. His battered face was incorporated into the story line with the following explanation: after working out at a Las Vegas gym, Hulk was attacked in the parking lot by a group of vicious thugs—a gang presumed to have been hired by Money, Inc. in a failed attempt to prevent Hulk from competing at *WrestleMania IX.* Throughout the match it was fairly obvious that most of the blows Hulk absorbed were below shoulder level so that no further damage would be inflicted on his face. DiBiase and Rotundo provided most of the match's energy and took most of the abuse. For Hulk, unfortunately, it was far from a typical performance. He spent only a few minutes in the ring, and even though he and Brutus Beefcake won the match, and Hulk got a nice pop with his post-match routine of posing and celebrating, it was obvious that he was in distress. I remember sitting at ringside and looking at Hulk's eye, and thinking, *It doesn't even look red. It just looks like a black hole.* That Hulk had performed at all was admirable; that his night was not yet over was unthinkable.

The main event was an obvious mismatch. Yokozuna was so large that he dwarfed Bret Hart. Somehow, though, Bret was able to gain the upper hand in the match. Yokozuna was knocked nearly unconscious after crashing into the bare metal of a turnbuckle that had been stripped of its protective padding, and it appeared that the Hit Man might successfully defend his title after all. But as Bret straddled Yokozuna and prepared to apply his patented move, the "sharpshooter," Yokozuna's manager, Mr. Fuji, tossed a handful of "Fuji Dust" (a mixture of salt and powder, I believe) into Bret's face, temporarily blinding the champion. This, of course, gave Yokozuna time to recover, and within a few moments he had pinned Bret and captured the World Wrestling Federation title.

But that was hardly the end of the show. As Bret lay writhing on the mat, Hulk Hogan, wearing his signature red tights and bright yellow cowboy boots, ran into the ring to assist his fallen friend. Then, as Hulk ushered Bret back to the dressing room, Mr. Fuji grabbed the microphone and began taunting Hulk, calling him, among other things, a "yellow American." Mr. Fuji offered Hulk a title shot—right then and there—and after getting a nod of approval from Bret Hart, Hulk accepted. As the crowd erupted, Hulk raced back into the ring. But as he and Yokozuna prepared to lock up, Mr. Fuji again

OPPOSITE: Yokozuna brings the Hit Man down to one knee.

grabbed a handful of Fuji Dust. This time, however, Hulk ducked, allowing the dust to hit Yokozuna. Blinded and unable to defend himself against a leg drop, the new champion hit the canvas and was quickly pinned. In a span of twenty-three seconds, from the start of the match to the closing bell, Hulk Hogan had miraculously become the Federation champion for the fifth time—and it happened in a match that was unscheduled and unpromoted.

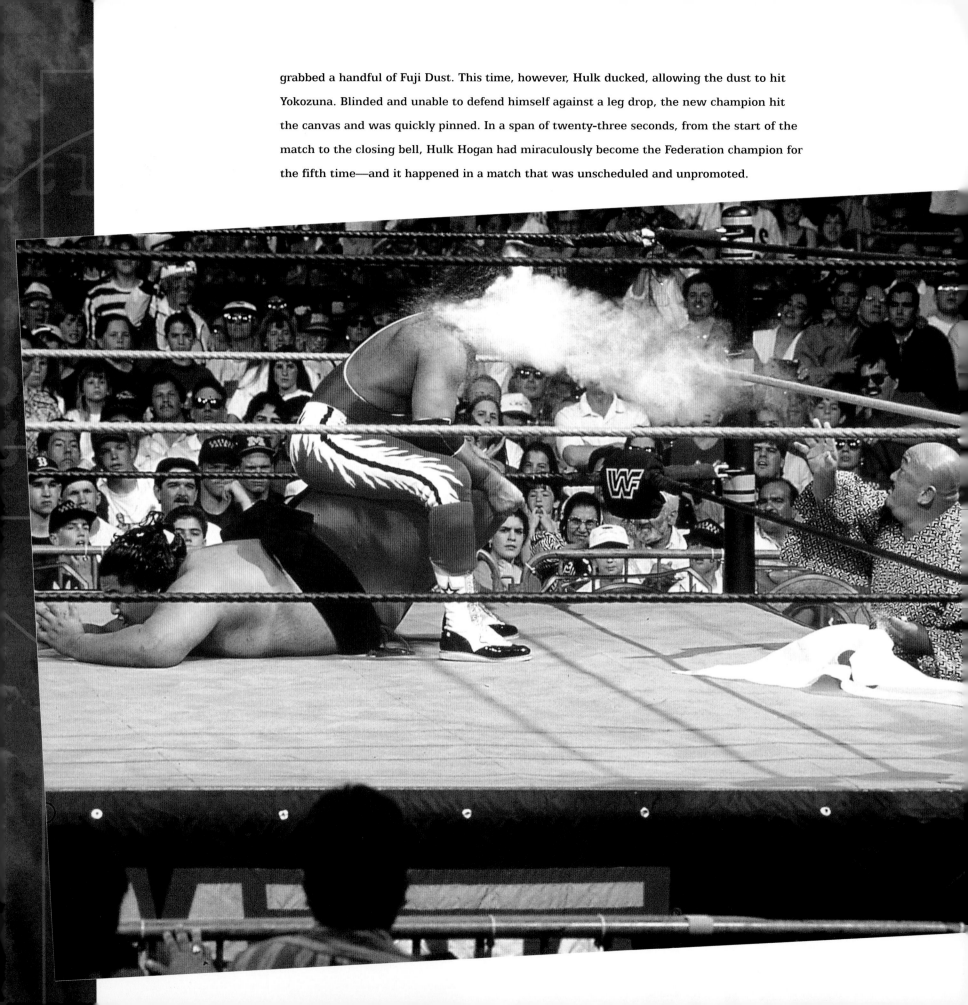

It's still unclear exactly how all of this came to pass, but my understanding is that on the day of *WrestleMania IX*, Hulk himself came up with the idea of making a dramatic comeback and leaving with the title. Before that, I think Bret Hart probably expected to leave *WrestleMania IX* as the champion. It was a weird twist, but there's no disputing its effectiveness. Everyone was caught completely by surprise. Twelve hours earlier I wasn't sure Hulk was even going to wrestle, and now he had wrestled twice and recaptured the championship! It was an extraordinary turn of events.

To me, though, the most memorable thing about *WrestleMania IX* was something that occurred after the match, as the stadium rocked and Hulk celebrated and posed. Vince McMahon, who had been supervising the production of the Pay-Per-View broadcast, ran down the entranceway in street clothes, slid under the ropes and into the ring, and in a genuine display of emotion, wrapped his arms around Hulk Hogan.

LEFT: Mr. Fuji hurls a fistful of powder into Hart's face.

ABOVE: Hogan shocks the audience with his fifth title win.

It was the first time anyone could remember Vince appearing out of character like that in the ring. When I asked him about it later, he said, "The emotion just took over. I was thinking, 'Happy days are here again.'"

That wasn't the case, of course. Hulk Hogan wasn't really part of the family again, and in fact this would be his final *WrestleMania* appearance. In that moment, though, the clock had been turned back. Hulk Hogan was champion of the World Wrestling Federation, and Vince McMahon was right by his side.

World Wrestling Federation Title Match:
Yokozuna (Champion—managed by Mr. Fuji & Jim Cornette)
vs. Bret "Hit Man" Hart
(with special referee Rowdy Roddy Piper)

Main Event Match:
Bret "Hit Man" Hart vs. Owen Hart

World Wrestling Federation Title Match:
Yokozuna (Champion—managed by Mr. Fuji & Jim Cornette)
vs. Lex Luger (with special referee Mr. Perfect)

Ladder Match for World Wrestling Federation Intercontinental Title:
Razor Ramon ("Champion")
vs. Shawn Michaels ("Champion")

Pinfalls Count Anywhere in the Arena Match:
Macho Man Randy Savage vs. Crush

World Wrestling Federation Tag Team Title Match:
Quebecers (Champions) vs. Men on a Mission

Mixed Tag Team Match:
Doink & Dink vs. Bam Bam Bigelow & Luna Vachon

Earthquake vs. Adam Bomb (managed by Harvey Wippleman)

World Wrestling Federation Women's Title Match:
Alundra Blayze (Champion) vs. Leilani Kai

For the tenth anniversary of

WrestleMania, the World Wrestling Federation returned to New York, to the very same building where the first *WrestleMania* had been held: Madison Square Garden. It was billed as "*WrestleMania X:* 10 Years in the Making." A prosaic slogan, perhaps, but nonetheless true, as the theme of this event was a retrospective look at the first nine *WrestleManias*.

WrestleMania X was nothing less than a celebration of the biggest event in sports-entertainment. It marked the birth of the World Wrestling Federation Fan Festival, a vastly expanded version of the event envisioned by Mark Etess several years earlier in Atlantic City. The Fan Festival lasted three days and included video game booths, autograph sessions, opportunities to interact with wrestlers . . . there was even a place where you could have your voice recorded as the announcer on a classic match.

The Fan Festival was immensely popular, primarily because it gave the fans a chance to meet the stars, which rarely happens at other big-time sports or entertainment events. You don't shake hands with Meryl Streep at the Oscars. You don't chat with Mike Krzyzewski at the Final Four. But at *Wrestle-Mania X,* the Fan Festival broke down the wall that naturally separates celebrities from the people who make them celebrities: the fans. The Fan Festival grew out of a desire to do something for our burgeoning audience, especially for those who would not be fortunate enough to see *WrestleMania* in person.

OPPOSITE: Lex Luger and Razor Ramon boost Bret "Hit Man" Hart after his win.

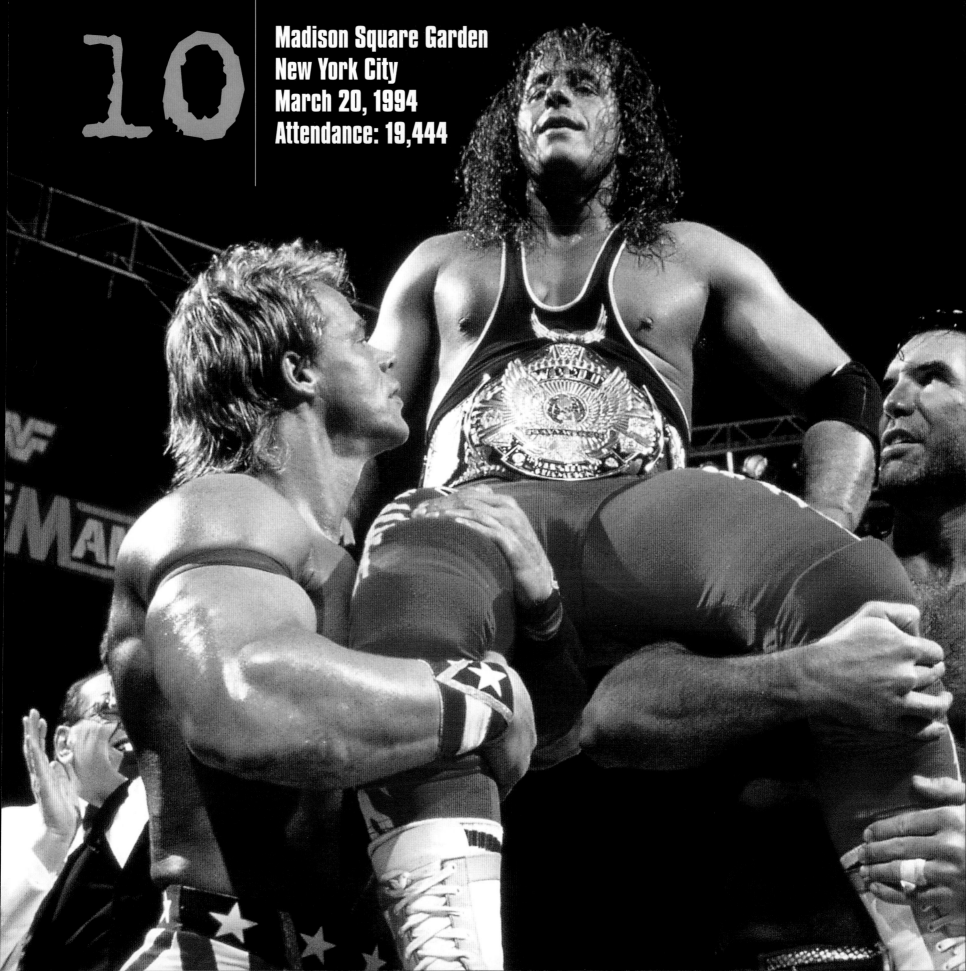

10

Madison Square Garden
New York City
March 20, 1994
Attendance: 19,444

There was never any doubt that we'd be able to sell out Madison Square Garden— that just wasn't an issue. The top-priced ticket to *Wrestle-Mania* by this point had reached three hundred dollars, which is pretty steep by any standard. Nevertheless, the entire building was sold out less one than hour after tickets went on sale. Every-one in the front office was under-standably pleased with that response, but there was a general consensus that something more could be done; for an event that was sold out months in advance, in a city like New York, it just didn't

make sense to limit access to the 20,000 people who would be at Madison Square Garden on March 20. The Fan Festival was the answer: eight two-hour sessions over the course of three days, with approximately 10,000 people attending each session.

To further serve the audience, closed-circuit tickets were sold to the Paramount Theater, a 5,000-seat arena that is located in the same building that houses the Madison Square Garden Arena. These fans, who paid twenty dollars to watch *WrestleMania X* on television only a few hundred feet from where the event was taking place, were provided a special treat: during the matches, Randy Savage took a walk through the tunnels and access routes of Madison Square Garden and appeared from behind the giant screen at the Paramount Theater. This was a complete surprise to the fans, and it was not something that had been planned far in advance. On the day of the event, when we realized there would be a huge closed-circuit turnout because so many people simply wanted to be near the action (after all, they could have simply ordered Pay-Per-View and enjoyed *Wrestle-Mania X* in the comfort of their own homes), it seemed like a good idea to give these diehard fans a bonus. And Randy was more than happy to oblige. When he stepped out in front of the audience, it naturally caused a big ruckus, but in a wholly positive way. Randy signed autographs, shook hands, and generally made everyone at the Paramount feel as though they were part of something special. Which, of course, they were.

OPPOSITE: A fan surveys Federation
action figures at the three-day
Fan Festival.

BELOW: Madison Square Garden was
sold out in less than an hour.

Where the Stars Come Out . . . Again

It's interesting to see what a difference a few years can make. *WrestleMania X* featured a gag involving a guy named Tim Watters, who is a Bill Clinton look-alike. The "President" was ushered to a skybox and interviewed during the event. The jokes and dialogue centered around a big scandal in the White House, which in this case was Mr. Clinton's tax problems. Small potatoes compared to what we've seen since, obviously, but it worked at the time.

After opting not to have a celebrity presence at *WrestleMania IX,* the World Wrestling Federation invited a number of stars to take part in the tenth anniversary celebration. Sy Sperling, well known as the owner of the Hair Club for Men, served as the official "hair consultant." Sy even went so far as to put a wig on ring announcer Howard Finkel. Midway through the show, to the delight of 20,000 screaming fans, Howard came out with a full head of hair that he clearly hadn't had earlier in the evening. It was just a silly little sight gag to provide some balance to the event—to give the audience a chance to breathe. Considering the intensity of some of the matches at *WrestleMania X,* this type of interlude was absolutely necessary.

Other celebrities who appeared at *WrestleMania X* included guest ring announcer Donnie Wahlberg, a member of the teen supergroup New Kids on the Block; timekeepers Jennie Garth, one of the stars of *Beverly Hills 90210,* and Rhonda Shear, buxom host of USA's popular late-night B-movie show *Up All Night;* and actor Burt Reynolds, who served as ring announcer for the final championship match. Burt has a reputation for sometimes being difficult, but he was absolutely great. He showed up and did his job in a completely professional and engaging manner, despite having a broken finger and a cast on his hand. Burt went to the ring several times, participated in everything he was asked to do, and was thoroughly gracious with everyone in the company. It's not an overstatement to say his performance could serve as a model for celebrity behavior at *WrestleMania.* Burt Reynolds "got it," which is all you can ask.

Sibling Rivalry

On a night that would include some of the most dramatic and unusual matches in *WrestleMania* history, it was appropriate that rock 'n' roll legend Little Richard opened the show with a unique and memorable version of "America the Beautiful." There is no one in popular music quite like Little Richard, and there had never been a *WrestleMania* quite like this one. Yokozuna held the championship belt heading into the event. Traditionally, the winner of January's Royal Rumble, a wild, thirty-man event in which wrestlers are eliminated by being tossed over the top rope, earns a trip to *WrestleMania* and a shot at the title. In 1994, though, the Royal Rumble had ended in a dead heat, with Bret Hart and Lex Luger, the final two combatants, flying out of the ring simultaneously. So, for the first time in history, it was decided that two men from the Royal Rumble would have an opportunity to challenge the champion at *WrestleMania*.

In setting up the main event, it was determined that Lex Luger would be the first man to face Yokozuna. Prior to that, though, Bret Hart would meet his younger brother, Owen, in what amounted to a grudge match. In that way, each of the three men involved in the main event would have to wrestle twice in order to win the title: Yokozuna would have to defeat Luger and Hart; Luger would have to beat Yokozuna and Hart; and Hart would have to face his brother and then defeat the winner of the Yokozuna-Luger match.

The match between Bret and Owen was, in a manner of speaking, one from the heart. According to the story line, the two brothers were embroiled in a feud, and Owen viewed this match as a chance to prove to the wrestling world that he was the more talented of the Hart siblings. It really was kind of poignant, since anyone who knew Bret and Owen understood how close they were, and that there was absolutely no bad blood between them at all. They were two of the finest technical wrestlers around. Both of them had grown up in the business, and you got the feeling that this was something they had always wanted to do, probably since they were little kids wrestling in the basement, one of them playing the bad guy, the other playing the good guy. On this night, Bret was the good guy, the hardworking wrestler who had fought long and hard for a chance to win the title, and who most fans probably felt deserved the belt. Owen was not a contender for the championship; he was the envious little brother intent less on winning the match than on injuring or exhausting Bret, and thus softening Bret up for Yokozuna. That Owen did, in fact, win the match was almost irrelevant.

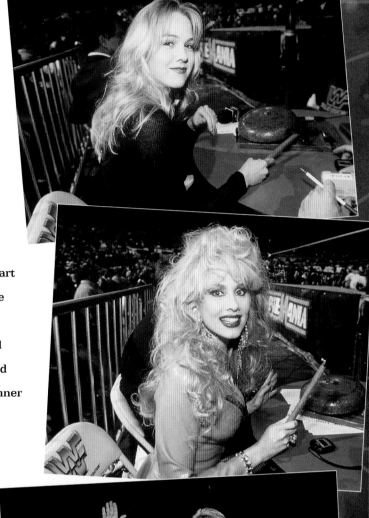

TOP AND CENTER: Teen heart-throb Jennie Garth and B-movie vixen Rhonda Shear took turns ringing the bell.

BOTTOM: Bill Clinton look-alike Tim Watters.

A New Champion For the second consecutive year, Yokozuna was compelled to wrestle twice for the championship. And for the second consecutive year, he left without the belt. After beating Lex Luger on a disqualification (Lex had assaulted the referee), Yokozuna met Bret Hart, who was clearly the crowd favorite. Before the match, as Bret was preparing to enter the ring, a small problem developed. Bret apparently had gotten word that his wife was not seated right at ringside, and he found this to be more than a little disturbing. So, he made it clear that he would not get back into the ring until his wife was moved to a ringside seat. The task of finding her fell to Toni Star-

LEFT: Owen Hart defeats his older brother Bret with the "Sharpshooter."

OPPOSITE: Yokozuna scored a win when rival Lex Luger attacked ref Mr. Perfect.

son, a longtime staffer. Unfortunately, Toni didn't know Bret's wife or where she was sitting, so it really was like looking for a needle in a haystack. Somehow, miraculously, Toni found Bret's wife (she was wearing a pink jacket that matched the colors of Bret's tights) and ushered her to a ringside seat. Placated, Bret jumped into the ring and went about the business of entertaining 20,000 fans.

For Yokozuna, the match ended in ignominy, with him tumbling in exhaustion from the top rope while trying to crush Bret with a "Banzai Splash." Bret covered the fallen giant and captured the elusive World Wrestling Federation title. Afterward, a frustrated and angry Yokozuna knocked Bret down, splashed him a few times, and left him dazed and horizontal, the championship belt stretched across his chest. Bret slowly recovered and struggled to his feet, exhausted but triumphant, and as he regained his strength, it seemed to be one of those pivotal moments in Federation history. Here was a new champion, a well-liked performer who probably should have won the title a year earlier, finally getting

his reward. But it was happening in a thoroughly atypical manner. The *WrestleMania* champion usually had the look of a superhero. He stood proudly, confidently in the middle of the ring and accepted the cheers and adulation of the fans. In this instance, however, the champion was exhausted and battered. He was a survivor. The reaction to this scenario was different, as well. The winner of *WrestleMania* typically stands alone. But as Bret wobbled in the ring with the belt held over his head, Lex Luger emerged to shake his hand. Then Burt Reynolds shook his hand. And Randy Savage. Eventually, all of the "good guys" in the Federation were in the ring with Bret, congratulating the new champion. Rather than a passing of the torch from one man to another, as we had seen with Hulk Hogan and the Ultimate Warrior, here was Bret Hart, in effect, accepting the torch from his co-workers. And this became the lasting image of Bret winning the title at *WrestleMania X.*

Climbing the Ladder

As unique and memorable as the main event was at *WrestleMania X,* it was not the most exciting match of the night. In fact, the thing I will remember most about *WrestleMania X* is a ladder match between Shawn Michaels and Razor Ramon, with the Intercontinental title on the line. This was supposed to be merely an undercard match, a teaser to the main event; it wound up being one of the most captivating, grueling, and unforgettable matches *WrestleMania* has ever produced.

We recognize, of course, that professional wrestling is a show, and that what happens in the ring is carefully scripted. That's why the preferred term in the new millennium is "sports-entertainment." Because of this designation, there is a tendency to overlook the danger involved. These guys are performers, yes . . . but they're also athletes, and what they do in the ring requires strength and courage, tempered with a bit of common sense. That wrestlers are involved in risky business was never more evident than in the ladder match at *WrestleMania X.*

The backstory was that Shawn Michaels and Razor Ramon both had laid claim to the Intercontinental title, and each had a belt in his possession. Which belt was legitimate and which was fraudulent was anyone's guess. And so, the two championship belts were suspended above the ring, about

Wrestlers and celebrities flood
  the ring to help the Hit Man
  revel in his triumph.

fifteen feet in the air, and a ten-foot aluminum ladder was placed at ringside. In concept, it was a very simple match: the first person to successfully climb the ladder and take possession of the belts would be declared the Intercontinental champion. When the match first started, I think a healthy portion of the audience thought they were witnessing a silly gimmick: *Oh, they're gonna knock each other around and it'll be kind of hard to get up the ladder.* No one could be prepared for the exhibition that followed, for the effort and energy that went into what many people consider to be one of the greatest matches in World Wrestling Federation history.

A clash for the next millennium: Razor Ramon's ladder match with Shawn Michaels.

Shawn Michaels and Razor Ramon used that ladder as a battering ram, as a bat. They did so many different things that simply could not have been practiced or pre-arranged. It was absolutely amazing. When you see a ten-foot ladder in the middle of a ring, and the ring is four feet off the ground, and a man starts climbing while another man tries to knock him down, you realize very quickly that someone could be seriously hurt. So there was an intensity to this match that I had never experienced. At one point, Shawn nearly reached the top of the ladder. He was reaching up to grab the belts when Razor, who had been down, summoned the strength to pursue his opponent once more. He climbed the ladder, grabbed Shawn by the back of his pants, and yanked him backward. Together they fell from a height of nearly ten feet, with the ladder tumbling after them. As they hit the mat and rolled over, a ripple of laughter spread through the arena: Shawn Michaels' tights had been pulled down around his knees! This pro-vided some much-needed comic relief, but within a few seconds the performers were back at it. Every time one of them clawed his way to the top rung of the ladder, you could feel the crowd holding its collective breath. It was one of those situations where you watch with your head turned ninety degrees away from the action, just sort of peeking with one eye because you really can't bear to watch, but you don't want to miss anything either.

It wasn't a brutal match in the traditional sense. There was no blood and no one was seriously injured. But it seemed that the potential for serious jeopardy was greater than in any other match I'd ever seen. It ended with both men climbing together, and Razor reaching the belts first. Then they both fell to the mat, exhausted

in a way that can't possibly be faked. This was definitely a match in which both par-ticipants were just barely able to roll out of the ring and stagger back to the dressing room. It was also the type of match that prompted not only cheers and applause, but gasps of disbelief. Most good matches entice the fans to participate—*WrestleMania,* after all, is a participatory event for the crowd. The wrestlers want that; they *need* it. But in this instance, the performance was so different, so intense, so—dare I say—real, that Razor Ramon and Shawn Michaels elicited a reaction unlike anything I had ever seen.

Once again, the World Wrestling Federation lit up the Great White Way.

WRESTLEMANIA XI

World Wrestling Federation Title Match:
Diesel (Champion—accompanied by Pamela Anderson)
vs. Shawn Michaels
(accompanied by Jenny McCarthy & bodyguard Sid)

Special Challenge Grudge Match:
Lawrence Taylor
vs. Bam Bam Bigelow

World Wrestling Federation Intercontinental Title:
Double J Jeff Jarrett
(Champion—with The Roadie in his corner)
vs. Razor Ramon (with The 1-2-3 Kid in his corner)

World Wrestling Federation Tag Team Title Match:
Smoking Gunns (Champions)
vs. Owen Hart & Mystery Partner

Special Attraction: "I Quit!" Match:
Bret "Hit Man" Hart
vs. Mr. Bob Backlund
(with special referee Rowdy Roddy Piper)

The Undertaker (managed by Paul Bearer)
vs. King Kong Bundy

Tag Team Match:
Lex Luger & British Bulldog
vs. Jacob & Eli Blu

With Hulk Hogan clearly out of the picture and a new generation of superstars emerging to take his place, *WrestleMania XI* was a transitional event for the World Wrestling Federation. The decision to bring the event to Hartford, the capital of the Federation's home state, was tied to the fact that Hartford was also scheduled to host the International Special Olympics in the summer of 1995. So *WrestleMania XI* really became the kickoff for the promotion of the Special Olympics. The press conference to announce that *WrestleMania* was coming to the Civic Center was attended by Connecticut Governor Lowell Weicker and actress Susan St. James, who was deeply involved in the Special Olympics and who had been a guest at *WrestleMania 2* nearly a decade earlier. Their presence naturally lent an air of credibility and mainstream acceptance to what had always been sort of a "fringe" event. After all, it wasn't all that long ago that we'd been compelled to set up our own ticket office at the Toronto SkyDome. Now we were being embraced by the governor of Connecticut and one of the most reputable charitable organizations around. Not only that, but *WrestleMania XI* also represented the first time the event had a national sponsor, in this case the toy manufacturer Tyco.

At the same time, the World Wrestling Federation found itself without a major superstar at the top of the company roster, someone who transcended the world of sports-entertainment, as Hulk Hogan had done in the 1980s, and Stone Cold Steve Austin and The Rock would do in the 1990s. The main event featured Shawn Michaels against Federation champion Diesel. In Diesel you had a

OPPOSITE: Bam Bam tries his intimidation tactics on Lawrence Taylor.

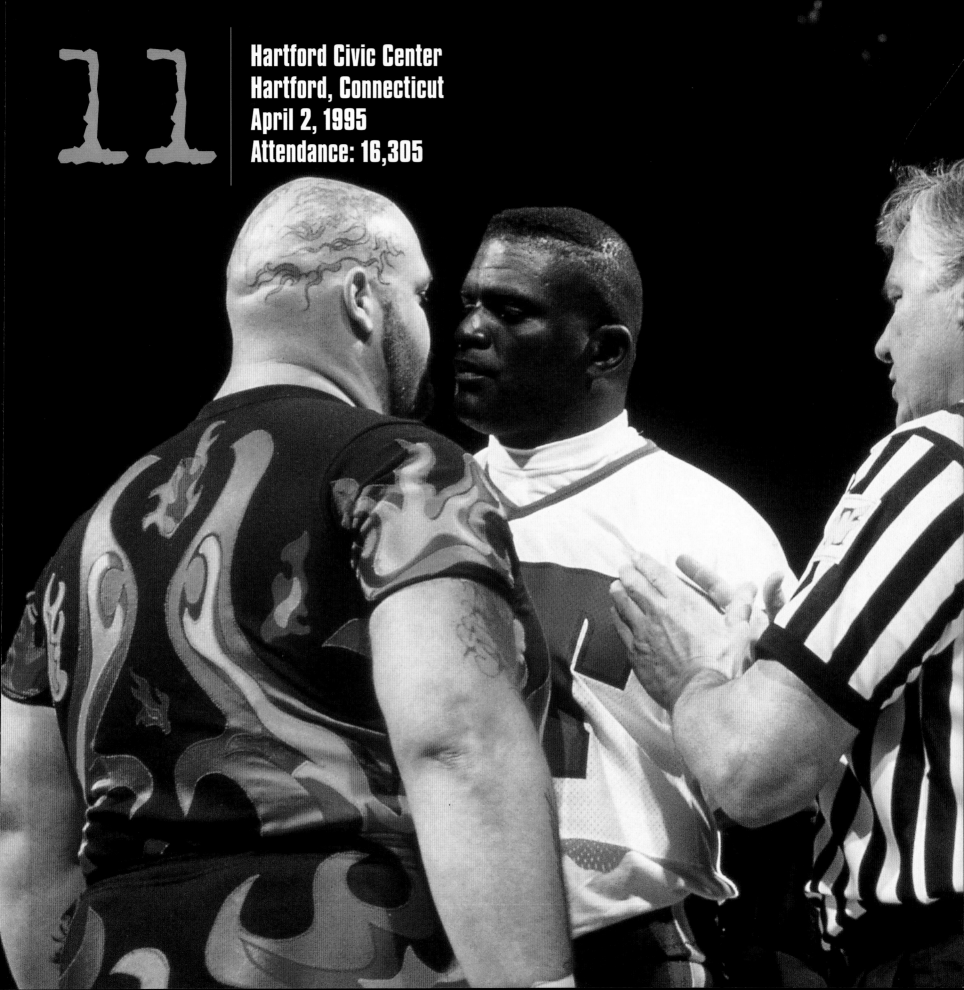

11

Hartford Civic Center
Hartford, Connecticut
April 2, 1995
Attendance: 16,305

guy who was a big physical specimen, and he did, to a degree, foreshadow the new attitude that the Federation would soon adopt; although he was not nearly as rough as many of the characters in today's World Wrestling Federation, his characterization leaned in that direction. Diesel was not a *bad* champion; he just wasn't a very memorable champion. He was sort of like William Henry Harrison, the ninth president of the United States, who died in office only one month after he was inaugurated. No one has ever said Harrison wasn't a good president. In the scheme of things, though, he just wasn't a very *important* president. In hindsight, Diesel was something of a placeholder.

Shawn Michaels, meanwhile, was an athletic performer who had the potential to become an extremely popular champion, but at this point he provoked different responses from the fans. Shawn wasn't necessarily a good guy or a popular guy. And he wasn't necessarily a heel. He was somewhere in the middle, still trying to find his character and his role within the company. In a sense, Shawn's appearance at *WrestleMania XI* was a rite of passage, like when a team goes to the Super Bowl for the first time . . . and loses. If that team is fortunate enough to return the next year, the players tend to be more confident, relaxed. Their attitude seems to be, "Last time we were just happy to be here. Now we know what it's all about." *WrestleMania XI* was a logical step in the career of Shawn Michaels. He had performed in a remarkable battle for the Intercontinental title at *WrestleMania X,* and now he was wrestling in the main event with the Federation championship belt at stake. For Shawn, perhaps, the most important thing about *WrestleMania XI* is that it prepared him and the fans for what would come next.

ABOVE: Federation kingpin Diesel gets a rise from sultry Pam Anderson.

OPPOSITE: Shawn Michaels keeps Diesel close to the mat.

Where Deals Are Made

Although there was nothing wrong with a main event that featured Shawn Michaels and Diesel, there was a general understanding that *WrestleMania XI* would benefit from an infusion of star power. The source of that power turned out to be Lawrence Taylor, the former all-pro football player for the New York Giants. L.T., as he was commonly known, was arguably the greatest linebacker in the history of the National Football League. He had a rare combination of size, speed, and intuition, and he played the game with unparalleled ferocity. L.T.'s propensity for living fast and hard had gotten him in trouble on occasion; nevertheless, he was genuinely revered not only by fans, but by his fellow athletes.

L.T. had been out of football for only a short time, so he remained an immensely popular and visible star. Vince, of course, knew all about Lawrence Taylor, and L.T. became the focus of the company's recruiting efforts. Vince had heard that Taylor was a fan of professional wrestling, but that did not necessarily mean he would want to take an active role at *WrestleMania XI;* and even if he was interested, there was some question as to whether he would be a good fit. Yes, Lawrence Taylor was one of the greatest athletes of his generation, but a lot of great athletes had failed miserably in the squared circle. Even in a limited role, there was no guarantee of success. As we had seen on previous occasions, some celebrities simply didn't understand what was expected of them at *WrestleMania,* and as a result their performances were neither entertaining nor inspiring.

In the case of Lawrence Taylor, there was sufficient excitement to warrant pursuing the matter further. Vince started out by going through Taylor's agent, but after a few weeks without progress, decided to take a different approach. Someone in our community relations department who had done a lot of work with football players made a few calls, and eventually found out that Lawrence would be hosting a charity golf tournament in the Northeast. So Lex Luger and a volunteer from the front office drove over and played in the tournament. The volunteer ended up driving L.T.'s golf cart that day, and before they even reached the first tee, the volunteer floated an idea.

"Look," she said. "I know you don't want to talk business, but we just want you to know that Vince would really like to talk to you about the possibility of doing something at *WrestleMania.*"

L.T.'s initial reaction was, "Well, we'll see. I'll think about it." But as Luger and L.T. spent the day on the golf course, interacting and chatting, L.T. warmed to the idea. By the time his round was complete, L.T. was excited about the possibility of participating in *WrestleMania.* "I'll have my agent call Vince," he said. Less than two days later the deal was done.

The Natural Of all the celebrities who have ever been involved in *WrestleMania,* no one has taken a more active role than Lawrence Taylor. He was more than just a celebrity—he was an athlete and a performer who fit in so well that one could almost imagine him having a second career as a professional wrestler. Certainly, other football players had participated in *WrestleMania* over the years—*WrestleMania* 2 had featured Chicago Bears star William "Refrigerator" Perry and several other NFL players. But that was pretty much limited to one day of involvement. Traditionally, the celebrities and athletes who were invited to participate in *WrestleMania* remained on the fringe of the promotion. They were there for entertainment value, to give the event depth and intrigue. When it came time to step into the ring, however, the celebrities generally became spectators. The handful of personalities who had been involved in matches had done so in a limited, carefully controlled way. Lawrence Taylor's role would be much different.

L.T.'s opponent at *WrestleMania XI* was Bam Bam Bigelow, a menacing, rotund man whose shaven head was adorned with tattoos. Rather than merely meeting Bam Bam in the ring on the night of *WrestleMania,* L.T. engaged in a three-month feud with his nemesis, beginning with a shoving match at the Royal Rumble in January. What made this interaction work so well was the secrecy that had surrounded it. L.T. was merely a spectator in the crowd. Other than Bam Bam, none of the wrestlers had any idea that the greatest linebacker in NFL history was about to join their ranks. After a tag team loss, Bam Bam walked to the front row, where Taylor had been sitting, and accused L.T. of heckling him. L.T. stood up, the men jawed at each other for a few seconds, and then Bam Bam thrust his fists into L.T.'s chest, knocking him backward. The crowd, of course, was shocked. It really caught everyone, including the rest of the performers and most of the office staff, by surprise, and it caused a great deal of excitement. It reminded me of when you watch the Slam-Dunk Contest at the NBA All-Star Game, and you see all these great ballplayers sitting on the sidelines, watching their co-workers flying and jamming all over the place. The players who aren't even involved suddenly become fans again—they're cheering and high-fiving and applauding, just like the people in the stands. When Bam Bam Bigelow shoved Lawrence Taylor, it prompted the same sort of reaction backstage among the World Wrestling Federation superstars. It was as if they were all saying, "Wow . . . this is gonna be cool!"

And it was. The buildup to *WrestleMania XI* focused heavily on the Bam Bam Bigelow–Lawrence Taylor grudge match, to the point that in a very real sense it did become the main event. L.T. was immersed in the promotion throughout the later winter months. A week before *WrestleMania XI,* a

A public workout in Times Square quickly degenerates into a brawl between Bam Bam and L.T.

public workout was held in New York's Times Square. A ring was constructed and traffic was stopped as a massive crowd turned out to watch L.T. train for his professional wrestling debut. Of course, they also showed up with the hope of seeing another clash between L.T. and Bam Bam Bigelow, and they weren't disappointed. The two engaged in another nose-to-nose shouting match that once again culminated in Bam Bam humiliating Taylor by shoving him to the ground. In New York, no less, where L.T. was almost royalty.

Predictably, the mainstream media viewed Lawrence Taylor's participation in *WrestleMania* as a serious fall from grace. *USA Today* did a cover story. It was mentioned in *Sports Illustrated*. And while it was nice to have L.T. acting as a conduit to the traditional sports media, it was distressing to see the way his role was regarded. The press seemed to be not just upset, but actually insulted that Lawrence Taylor would "stoop" to taking part in a professional wrestling match.

BELOW: Taylor zaps Bigelow with a perfectly executed forearm smash.

OPPOSITE: Bam Bam finds himself trapped in L.T.'s bulldog headlock.

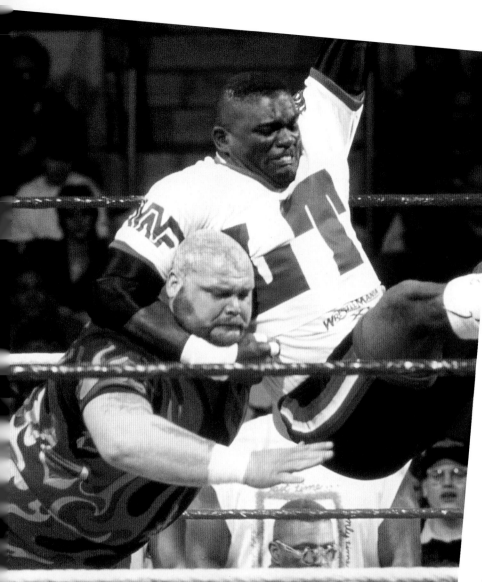

Part of this, I think, could be traced back to L.T.'s unusual relationship with the fans and media. His well-documented problems with drugs and alcohol had made him something of a fallen hero, but then he had redeemed himself. The constant in his life was football—he had always been a sensational linebacker, regardless of his troubles off the field. Confusing matters even further was his relationship with Giants coach Bill Parcells, a noted taskmaster who exacted supreme effort from his players. Parcells was a former West Point coach, and one would have expected him to demand that his players remain on the straight and narrow. But he loved Lawrence Taylor, a man who some people say redefined the position of linebacker, but who also was a renegade off the field. So, mixed emotions greeted L.T. wherever he went; the media, especially, were unsure whether to hate him or love him. Was he arrogant? Reckless? Or was he a gifted athlete and competitor who deserved another chance? At various times he seemed to be all of those things. But when he became, briefly, a professional wrestler, the reaction from the press was unduly harsh. It was as if he had personally disappointed the writers, editors, and broadcasters who control the media in this country. They branded him a loser . . . which was completely unfair.

Stealing the Show Few World Wrestling Federation events have featured as much celebrity voltage as *WrestleMania XI*. The popular R&B group Salt-N-Pepa sang "America the Beautiful"; teen actor Jonathan Taylor Thomas was the guest timekeeper; NFL stars Carl Banks, Rickey Jackson, Ken Norton, Steve McMichael, Chris Spielman, and Reggie White backed up Lawrence Taylor; and actor Nicholas Turturro of *NYPD Blue* served as a ring announcer and reporter. Turturro, one of the first guest announcers ever given an opportunity to do backstage interviews, was involved in an interesting example of fact blending with fiction. His "job" was to track down breaking stories, the biggest of which was the search for *Baywatch* babe Pamela Anderson. Anderson was one of two stars (the other was *Playboy* playmate Jenny McCarthy) vying for the privilege of escorting the champion, Diesel, into the ring for his match against Shawn Michaels. According to the story line, Anderson was missing, and Turturro's assignment was to find out what had happened to her. Coincidentally, Anderson really did get delayed on her way to the event. The Hartford Civic Center is a unique site that includes a hotel, shopping mall, convention center, and arena. On the night of *WrestleMania XI*, of course, the entire complex was mobbed with fans. To avoid the throng, the celebrities and wrestlers were supposed to take a service elevator from the hotel to a lower level in the building where they would then be escorted by security into the arena. Unfortunately, the service elevator was not working, so Pamela Anderson, queen of the pinup and soon-to-be-queen of the Internet, had to walk from the hotel to the arena, through thousands of screaming fans. It was not exactly the best way to do things, and it caused her to be significantly late. Meanwhile, Nicholas Turturro was filing reports on her absence, not realizing that she actually did endure an unrelated and unscripted difficulty in trying to get to the arena.

TOP: Stunners Pam Anderson and Jenny McCarthy charm Nicholas Turturro.

LEFT: Salt-N-Pepa headed Lawrence Taylor's cheerleading squad.

There were some interesting matches at *WrestleMania XI,* including Diesel's victory over Shawn Michaels for the Federation championship and The Undertaker's match against King Kong Bundy. One of the more memorable moments of the evening, in fact, came in the latter event, when The Undertaker, who at six-foot-nine and more than three hundred pounds is one of the biggest men in the company, climbed to the top rope in the corner, as if he were going to grab the turnbuckle and launch himself at his opponent—a fairly traditional move in the business. But The Undertaker did something that surprised everyone: he proceeded to walk along the top rope until he reached the middle of the side of the ring. Then he paused, bounced, and flew out over the ring, finally landing on top of his fallen opponent, doing what had to be one of the most inspired maneuvers of the evening.

There is no question, though, that *WrestleMania XI* belonged to Lawrence Taylor. That the script might call for L.T. to beat Bam Bam Bigelow probably wasn't a huge surprise; but the quality of his performance was stunning. L.T. not only flew off the top rope, he perfectly executed a back suplex, a move that takes most wrestlers years to perfect. He kicked out of Bam Bam's diving head butt; he drilled his opponent with a flying fist and a tackle to set up a pin.

No other celebrity, with the possible exception of Mr. T in the first *WrestleMania,* had so completely immersed himself in the promotion and been so willing to put his body at risk. Lawrence Taylor accepted a leading role and then did the work necessary to carry it off. More than that, really. He performed at a level far beyond what you would reasonably expect of a nonprofessional. But it wasn't easy for him. As Lawrence hobbled from the ring after his match, there was some initial concern that he had sustained some sort of injury. Not so. He was simply and utterly exhausted, to the point that he could barely walk. Like most people who have no experience with wrestling, L.T. didn't realize how difficult a match could be. At the highest level of sports-entertainment, twenty minutes in the ring can seem like a lifetime.

ABOVE: Jonathan Taylor Thomas seems unspooked by eerie Paul Bearer.

BELOW: An exhausted L.T. is helped from the ring after his win.

Iron Man Match for the World Wrestling Federation Title:

Bret "Hit Man" Hart (Champion) vs. Shawn Michaels (with his mentor Mexican wrestling star Jose Lothario)

The Undertaker (managed by Paul Bearer) vs. Diesel

Ultimate Warrior vs. Hunter Hearst Helmsley

Stone Cold Steve Austin vs. Savio Vega

Hollywood Back Lot Brawl:

Rowdy Roddy Piper vs. Goldust

Six-Man Tag Team Match:

Yokozuna, Ahmed Johnson & Jake "The Snake" Roberts vs. Vader, British Bulldog & Owen Hart

World Wrestling Federation Tag Team Title Match:

The Godwinns (managed by Hillbilly Jim) vs. Body Donnas (managed by Sunny)

Geriatric Match:

Huckster vs. Nacho Man

If *WrestleMania XI*, brimming with celebrities both in and out of the ring, showcased the World Wrestling Federation as a pop culture phenomenon, then *WrestleMania XII* represented a more traditional approach. Not that it lacked wit or hyperbole—as always, there was plenty of that; however, perhaps more than any other previous event, the focus of *WrestleMania XII* was clearly on the physical talent of the participants in the ring.

By this time the direction of the Federation in general and *WrestleMania* in particular had taken a definite turn toward the overtly athletic. The performers were becoming bigger, stronger, quicker, more agile . . . more inventive. Lawrence Taylor had done a terrific job the previous year, but as the product changed and the performers at the top of the roster became increasingly athletic, the notion of involving celebrities at *WrestleMania* lost a bit of its appeal. If the celebrity talent served no other purpose than window dressing, it almost detracted from the event—at least during this period of the World Wrestling Federation. So *WrestleMania XII* became the first *WrestleMania*

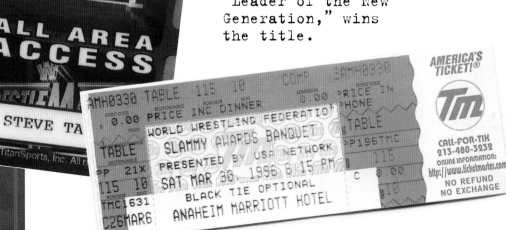

BELOW: The outrageous Slammy Awards preceded *WrestleMania XII*.

OPPOSITE: Shawn Michaels, "Leader of the New Generation," wins the title.

12

Arrowhead Pond
Anaheim, California
March 31, 1996
Attendance: 18,853

to be sold exclusively on the strengths of the product itself—on the performers. There were no guest competitors, no celebrities serving as announcers or broadcasters or timekeepers. In fact, there wasn't even a guest vocalist to sing "America the Beautiful." This was the World Wrestling Federation, on its own.

Ironically, the first *WrestleMania* to eschew stars from the entertainment industry was held in Anaheim, California, not far from Los Angeles. So, even though *WrestleMania XII* did not have a celebrity presence, there was a variety of ancillary events that offered a taste of Hollywood. For example, on Saturday, the day before *WrestleMania*, there was a big celebrity softball game to raise money for cystic fibrosis.

BELOW: Mexican great Jose Lothario massages Michaels's shoulders before his clash with Hart.

OPPOSITE: The Hit Man and the Heartbreak Kid ignite the Arrowhead Pond.

A team of Federation performers played against a team of celebrities that included television stars Jason Gedrick (then appearing on *Murder One*) and Jonathan Silverman, who portrayed the central character in the sitcom *The Single Guy*. More than 6,000 fans showed up to watch the game and everyone had a lot of fun. It was a worthwhile charity event that received some significant coverage in the Los Angeles media and gave *WrestleMania* a little of that Hollywood sheen. But it was an event that had very little connection to *WrestleMania* itself, and there was a conscious effort to make it that way.

An Awards Show with Attitude

On the eve of *WrestleMania* the World Wrestling Federation presented its own take on that peculiar American phenomenon known as the awards show. An odd and irreverent cross between the Emmys and the Grammys, the "Slammy Awards" show was broadcast nationally on USA Network. Fans had voted in a number of categories, including favorite wrestler, favorite match, and favorite theme song. One of the more interesting and, as it turned out, prescient categories was "best entrance." In an eerie foreshadowing of the next day's show, the fans gave this award to the Heartbreak Kid, Shawn Michaels. Shawn also was voted "Leader of the New Generation," the performer fans believed was most likely to become the next big superstar. Shawn was scheduled to meet Federation champion Bret Hart in the main

event at *WrestleMania XII*, and it was interesting to see that our fans obviously had some idea what would transpire. Shawn Michaels would indeed make one of the most memorable entrances in *WrestleMania* history, and he would leave with the Federation championship belt. And this was precisely what the fans had wanted to see, as indicated by the results of this poll, which had in fact taken place weeks earlier. Which event prompted the other? Well, that's like asking which came first, the chicken or the egg? I can't tell you, because I'm not really sure. All I can tell you is that when a story line works well, it's hard to tell where fact ends and fiction begins.

OPPOSITE: By Christmas Day, *WrestleMania XII* had been sold out.

BELOW: Bret "Hit Man" Hart makes Shawn Michaels groan on the mat.

The Slammy Awards included at least one other interesting example of life crashing into the soap opera that is the World Wrestling Federation story line. The event was set up like a typical awards show, with a stage at the front of the room and tables filled with Federation superstars and some local celebrities and presenters. At the time, we had a recurring character named Billionaire Ted, rather obviously a parody of Ted Turner, whose World Championship Wrestling organization was the most significant competitor to the World Wrestling Federation. The WCW was still in its infancy at the time, but already there was a pretty heated battle, with each organization raiding the other for talent. The Slammys represented a golden opportunity to needle the Mouth of the South, but it also led to some uncomfortable moments for at least one Federation superstar. Diesel, who had lost the title to Bret Hart a few months earlier, had already agreed to a deal with the WCW. *WrestleMania XII* would be his last World Wrestling Federation event. After that, he would be employed by Ted Turner. Well, Diesel was understandably (and hilariously) unnerved when he was assigned a seat next to the character of Billionaire Ted at the Slammy Awards. It was a good gimmick to put the two together, but I don't think anyone was prepared for Diesel to be quite so shaken by the joke. When he approached the table and spotted

Billionaire Ted, Diesel stopped, stared, and walked away. The former Federation champion
refused to sit with Billionaire Ted, presumably out of fear that he would offend his new
boss. I found that to be an interesting response: wrestlers, who are used to putting their
bodies on the line in the course of what often are dangerous and athletic performances, and
who will take emotional and physical beatings in front of millions of people, pretty much
on a daily basis, and who will agree to do a lot of stuff the average guy just wouldn't agree
to . . . these guys do draw the line at some point and say, "No! I won't do that." In Diesel's
case, the line was no different from the line drawn by employees all over the world. He had
a new job, and he was afraid of losing it. As Stone Cold Steve Austin might say, "That's the
bottom line."

The Ringmaster Speaking of Stone Cold Steve Austin, his *WrestleMania* debut came in Anaheim, although he was not yet the performer who would become one of the biggest and most popular wrestlers in history. In fact, if you had seen the advance promotional material for *WrestleMania XII,* you would have had a hard time finding any reference to Stone Cold Steve Austin. That's because this was the first time tickets for *WrestleMania* were available exclusively via mail order, which signaled a fairly significant change in demand for the event. While *Wrestle-Mania* had always sold out, prior to 1996 tickets had been made available through customary channels. As with any concert or sporting event, they could be purchased at the box office or by phone through a distributor such as TicketMaster. Now, though, some sort of interaction with the World Wrestling Federation was required in order to get tickets. You had to obtain an order form from our office, and then you had to mail the order form.

Any concerns that this strategy might alienate some fans were quickly laid to rest. Tickets for *WrestleMania XII* went on sale in November; by Christmas Day the event was sold out. This feverish response was at once humbling and thrilling. Instinctively, I knew the event's popularity was soaring, but I didn't realize how much until I reflected back on the days of *Wrestle-Mania 2,* when Big John Studd had been ready to put me through a wall because he was upset about the type of newspaper ads we were running. We had to aggressively market tickets then, and we did everything necessary to put fans in the seats. Now, suddenly, it was simply a matter of sending out a mail-order form. And it was only the beginning. Four years later *WrestleMania* would return to the Pond, and this time tickets would be available basically by invitation only.

The one drawback to promoting and selling out *Wrestle-Mania XII* so far in advance was the risk of distributing material that would be dated by the time of the event. Generic material—"See all the Superstars at *WrestleMania!*"—was used as often as possible in November and December, and even into early January. At some point, though, the specific performers, if not the exact matches, had to be promoted. That's why a spe-

TOP: Steve Austin, then called the Ringmaster, shoots Savio Vega toward the arena floor.

BOTTOM: Ref Tim White checks on Vega as he's caught in Austin's sleeper hold.

cial *WrestleMania XII* section in the *Orange County Register,* prepared in January, originally referred to Steve Austin as the "Ringmaster." Fortunately, the section wasn't scheduled to be published until March, and by that time we were able to correct the material and reflect the fact that the Ringmaster had become Stone Cold Steve Austin. The character was embryonic, but in his victory over Savio Vega, Steve Austin, with his goatee, shaved head, and trademark black trunks, displayed the gritty style that would lead him to superstardom.

On the Run

Shawn Michaels against Bret Hart was the centerpiece of *WrestleMania XII,* and indeed it had all the elements necessary for a truly dramatic match. But if you look at any *WrestleMania* in its entirety—if you think of it as a three-hour roller-coaster ride—then you realize that the undercard matches and various comedic interludes all play vital roles as well. In this case, when celebrity interaction probably wouldn't work, something else had to be devised to take the crowd through the emotional highs and lows expected of a *WrestleMania* experience. The answer was a Hollywood Back-Lot Brawl between Goldust and Roddy Piper.

The encounter, which was displayed on a giant screen for the audience at the Pond, began with Goldust arriving at a movie studio in a gold Cadillac and running down Roddy Piper. After recovering, Roddy responded by taking a baseball bat to Goldust's Caddy. Much mayhem ensued, of course, with each man utilizing as weapons the myriad props available on a back lot. After beating each other senseless for a while, the two engaged in a low-speed chase across the freeways of Los Angeles, Goldust in his Cadillac and Roddy in—what else?—a white Ford Bronco. This obviously evoked memories of O. J. Simpson's most famous run—his flight from police in 1994 after his wife was found murdered.

Helicopters followed Roddy and Goldust as they cruised toward Anaheim, capturing the chase on camera for millions of fans at home, as well as for the live audience. Although the World Wrestling Federation now routinely broadcasts action from outside the ring on the Titantron, it was a relatively new technique in 1996. And in fact, this was the match that proved to us that it not only could work, but could work brilliantly. The Back-Lot Brawl provided a break

BELOW: Piper swings for the fences in his Hollywood Back-Lot Brawl with Goldust.

BOTTOM: Prior to their freeway chase, Piper splatters Goldust across his Cadillac.

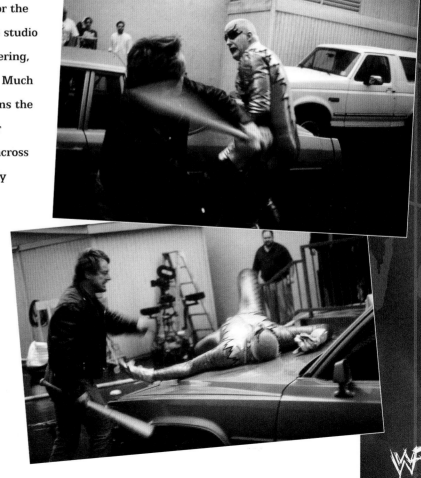

ABOVE: Goldust strangles the Rowdy One with a foreign object.

OPPOSITE: The Heartbreak Kid rockets off the ropes at the Hit Man.

from the intense nature of the overall event, and although it was hardly a comedy skit, it did make people laugh. It really had all the ingredients of a mini action-adventure movie.

After a while, the combatants arrived at the Pond, and the brawl reached its climax in the ring. The match ended with Roddy humiliating Goldust by stripping the flamboyant wrestler of his clothing and exposing his garters and nylons. Afterward, anyone who saw Roddy could tell he was completely spent. Near collapse, he had given one of the most difficult performances of his career. In truth, few people could have pulled it off. Roddy had an ability to maintain a high level of intensity that was matched by very few wrestlers. Physically, emotionally, athletically, he had a knack for performing at a peak for an extended period of time. He was better at that than perhaps anyone I've ever seen.

Hart to Heart When Shawn Michaels was introduced before the main event, 18,000 people turned toward the dressing room, fully expecting the sort of dramatic entrance for which the Heartbreak Kid was known. But as Shawn's music played, nothing happened. The fans began to look around for the challenger. There was a buzz in the building, as if everyone knew something special was about to happen. And then, as if straight out of a *Superman* movie, someone pointed up at the ceiling. The whole crowd looked up, and you could hear the *ooohhhs* and *aaahhhs* as Shawn appeared in the rafters of the Pond. Then, amid flashing lights, music, and fireworks, Shawn made a long, graceful entrance, floating toward the ring on a wire with his arms spread wide, as if flying. As his boots touched the floor, just outside the ring in a sea of adoring fans, you couldn't help but be struck by the realization that Shawn Michaels synthesized many of the best elements of professional wrestling's flashiest wrestlers, dating all the way back to Gorgeous George. He wore a highly ostentatious outfit, a formfitting tux with sequins; he had long, flowing hair and matinee idol looks; at the same time, Shawn was a gifted athlete, probably one of the most finely conditioned performers in the World Wrestling Federation. More than any other wrestler of that era, Shawn provoked emotional responses from the fans. Whether he was loved by women and admired by men, or admired by women and despised by men, it really didn't matter. Everyone had an opinion about Shawn Michaels. And that's crucial to the success of the main event at *WrestleMania*.

Being a more traditional performer, and one of the most proficient technical wrestlers in the business, Bret Hart opted for an entrance that

ABOVE: The Heartbreak Kid makes an unforgettable entrance into the arena.

OPPOSITE: The Hit Man basks in the spotlight as he leaves the dressing room.

was short on style and long on substance. He marched down the aisle and paused at ring-side, where his six-year-old son was seated. He removed his trademark "Hit Man" sunglasses, put them on his son, and climbed into the ring. The entrances perfectly reflected the contrast in styles of the two performers, and beautifully set up the main event.

Although there was great competitiveness between Bret and Shawn, there also existed a deep respect. It would be wrong to characterize the main event as a babyface match, primarily because the characters elicited vastly different reactions from the fans— Bret was all business; Shawn was a strutter . . . cool and cocky—but the animosity that naturally arises in the promotion of the main event at *WrestleMania* was noticeably absent. In fact, the promotion repeatedly touched on the theme of mutual respect, in terms of both men being very athletic and having a great deal of technical ability. Each character wanted the title, but neither was willing to denigrate his opponent.

Appropriately enough, considering the participants' backgrounds and abilities, *WrestleMania XII* represented the first time that the main event was an "iron man" match. In the old days of professional wrestling, it was common for the announcer to step into the ring and say something like, "This match is for the World Wrestling Federation championship, with a one-hour time limit." Since then, of course, time limits had fallen out of fashion. Television required commercial breaks, and the attention span of the audience was generally considered to be too short to handle a one-hour match. On this one occasion, however, it seemed to make sense to bring back a vestige of the past. So this became a sixty-minute championship match. A pin at the five-minute mark . . . or the ten-minute mark . . . or the twenty-minute mark . . . would not bring an end to the proceedings. The match would last precisely one hour, at the conclusion of which the wrestler with the most decisions—by pinfall, disqualification, submission . . . whatever—would be declared the winner and the Federation champion.

You might ordinarily expect four or five decisions in a sixty-minute time frame, but this event ended without a single decision. The most dramatic moment came in the final seconds, when Bret applied his famous "sharpshooter" hold on Shawn. The sharpshooter is a submission hold, and as the clock wound down, with the crowd counting off the seconds, *WrestleMania* felt more than ever like a traditional sporting event. Here we had Bret driving

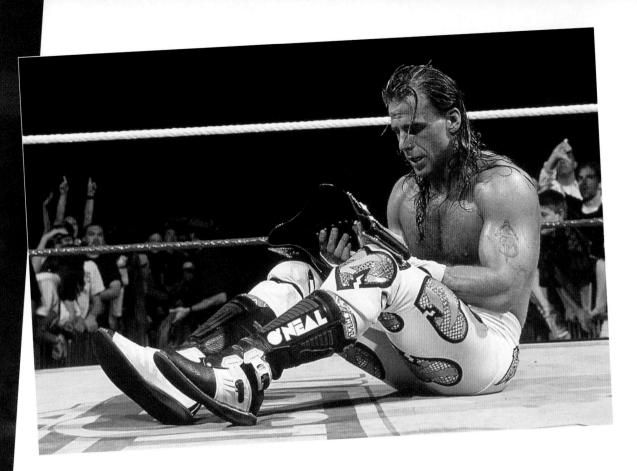

for the win, as if he was a yard away from a touchdown with the clock running out, and the referee, Earl Hebner, right there, waiting for the submission.

But it never came. Shawn Michaels held on and the clock ran out. The match was declared a draw, which meant Bret retained his title. So Bret picked up his championship belt and headed back up the aisle, only to be summoned back into the ring. The Federation's president, Gorilla Monsoon, had ruled that this particular match could not end in a draw, and therefore, to use another football analogy, it was time for sudden death. The first person to win by pin fall would be the champion.

After arguing for a bit, Bret returned to the ring. He seemed distracted, disoriented, and quickly fell victim to one of Shawn Michaels's favorite moves, the "super kick." The blow knocked Bret off his feet and onto the mat, where he was covered by the Heartbreak Kid. And so *WrestleMania XII* became not only the fulfillment of Shawn Michaels's lifelong dream—to become the Federation champion—but the fulfillment of the prophecies of fans around the country. The Heartbreak Kid had made a grand entrance and a spectacular exit. He was, indeed, the Leader of the New Generation.

LEFT: Michaels desperately grasps the rope, as Hart lifts and twists.

ABOVE: Shawn's lifelong dream is realized as he contemplates the belt.

World Wrestling Federation Title Match:
Sycho Sid (Champion) vs. The Undertaker

Submission Match:
Bret "Hit Man" Hart vs. Stone Cold Steve Austin
(with special guest referee Ken Shamrock)

Chicago Street Fight Match:
Ahmed Johnson & The Legion of Doom
vs. Faarooq & The Nation of Domination

World Wrestling Federation Tag Team Title Match:
Owen Hart & British Bulldog (Champions)
vs. Vader & Mankind (with Paul Bearer)

Special Attraction:
Goldust (managed by Marlena)
vs. Hunter Hearst Helmsley (with Chyna)

World Wrestling Federation Intercontinental Title Match:
Rocky Maivia (Champion)
vs. The Sultan (with Bob Backlund & The Iron Sheik)

Four-Team Elimination Tag Team Match:
Doug Furnas & Philip LaFon vs. The Godwinns
vs. Headbangers vs. New Blackjacks

In January 1997, when more than 60,000 fans packed the Alamodome in San Antonio, Texas, to watch hometown hero Shawn Michaels in the Royal Rumble, the promotion for *WrestleMania 13* seemed to be sailing along. The Heartbreak Kid was at the absolute height of his popularity—his presence in the Rumble helped the World Wrestling Federation set an Alamodome attendance record—and there was no doubt that he was going to be the headliner at *WrestleMania 13.* However, thirteen being an unlucky number (and a number with dramatic, theatrical implications, which is why the Roman numeral was not used), maybe it's no great surprise that things did not work out quite as planned. Shawn Michaels sustained an injury at the Royal Rumble, creating a chain reaction that made this one of the most challenging promotions in *WrestleMania* history. For three months the main event kept changing as we waited to see whether Shawn might return to the ring and other story lines played themselves out.

Selling out the event wasn't an issue—*WrestleMania* had become such a popular event that we were virtually guaranteed a sellout well in advance, regardless of who would be appearing on the card. *WrestleMania* had a life of its own now, just like the Super Bowl or World Series, or any big-time annual entertainment event. People simply wanted to be a part of it. But there's no denying that circumstances conspired against the promotion, and that this *WrestleMania* lacked the galvanizing effect that comes from a steady three-month buildup. With Shawn Michaels, the star of the moment, on the sideline, *WrestleMania 13* became a transitional event, one that featured a compelling match between two veterans in the main event, and on the undercard, stirring performances by two men who would soon reach a level of stardom previously achieved only by the likes of Hulk Hogan.

OPPOSITE: Stone Cold Steve Austin came into his own against Bret "Hit Man" Hart.

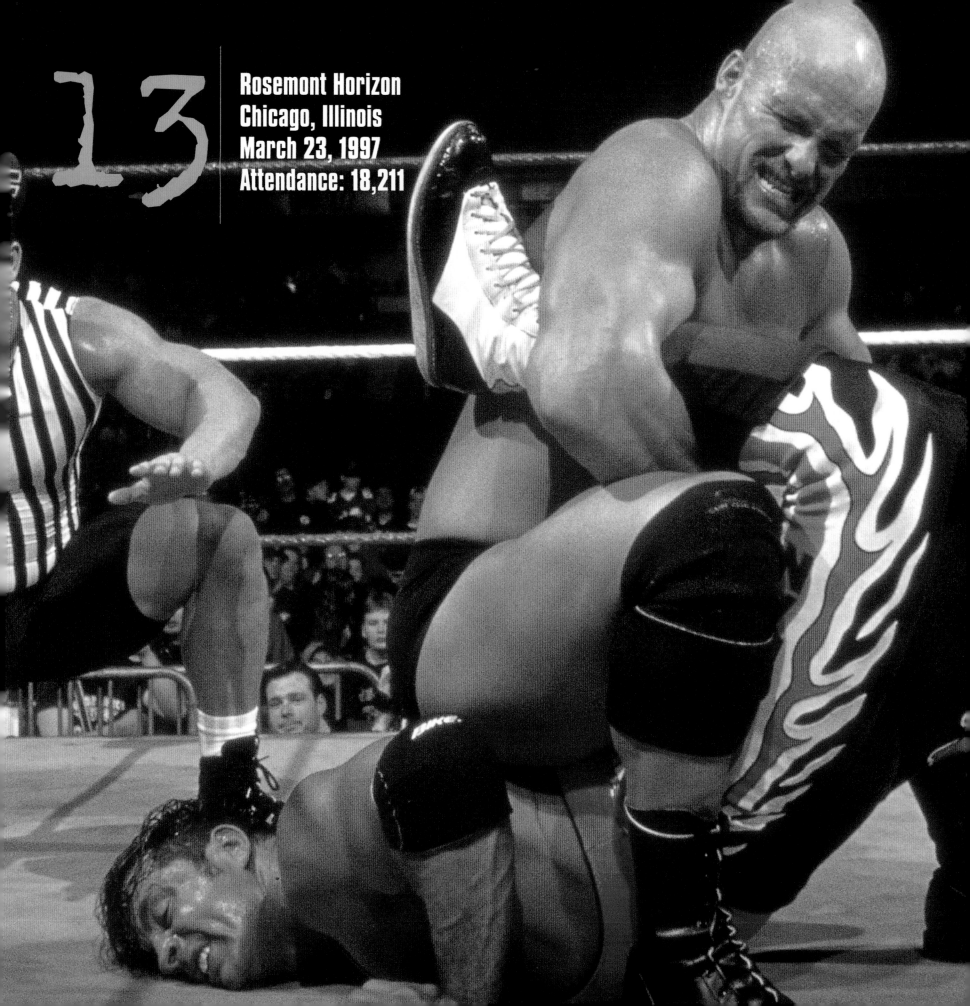

13

Rosemont Horizon
Chicago, Illinois
March 23, 1997
Attendance: 18,211

The Undertaker Rises to the Occasion Because

WrestleMania 13 did not have a clear, specific story line, it became a collection of important events and snapshots. And while it might not stand out as the most important *WrestleMania*, in retrospect, we can see it as an event that reflected a convergence of all the different eras of *WrestleMania*. We see the emergence of Stone Cold Steve Austin as the take-no-crap antihero; the introduction of the babyface Rocky Maivia, the third-generation wrestler making his *WrestleMania* debut; the Honky Tonk Man making an appearance as a guest ring announcer; the return of Captain Lou Albano; and Vince McMahon, resplendent in his tux, still playing the character of an over-the-top announcer, but about to become "Mr. McMahon," the Machiavellian corporate leader.

In the weeks and months leading up to *WrestleMania 13,* however, the burden of promotion fell primarily on the sturdy shoulders of The Undertaker, who would meet newly crowned champion Sycho Sid in the main event. This was surely one of the more confusing main events in the annals of *WrestleMania.* Sid and The Undertaker were two of most imposing physical specimens in the company, each about six-foot-eight and three hundred pounds. The Undertaker was, to put it mildly, an unconventional hero. I mean, it's hard to imagine that a character named The Undertaker would be cheered by the fans, but that's the way it turned out, primarily because his opponent was, as the name implied, a psychotic brute deserving little or no sympathy.

The Undertaker was one of the steadiest and most reliable performers in the Federation. He had risen to the level of champion on one previous occasion, but his character was sufficiently dark and reticent that it was hard to imagine him as the person who would carry the company for any length of time. The "Phenom," or "Dead Man," as The Undertaker was sometimes called, was merely a characterization, but like so many of the best characterizations

LEFT: The Undertaker and champion Sycho Sid engage in a stare-down.

OPPOSITE: The Man from the Dark Side chokeslams the titlist.

in sports-entertainment, there were similarities between the man and the monster who claimed he could steal the souls of his opponents. Away from the ring, The Undertaker was a soft-spoken man, less talkative than most—certainly less talkative than most professional wrestlers. Like the character he portrayed, he was a man of few words, and when he did choose to speak, he delivered his message in a deep, strong monotone. While he may not have had any firsthand experience with the afterlife, I don't think it was a big stretch for The Undertaker to portray a big, menacing character who preferred to let his talent do the talking.

Similarly, Sid had a little in common with the character he portrayed. While Sycho Sid was unpredictable, violent, and utterly mad in the ring, the man behind the character was one of the more unreliable guys in the World Wrestling Federation in terms of his responsibilities outside the ring. During the weeks leading up to *WrestleMania 13,* this caused a fair amount of anxiety for everyone involved. Had he not gotten hurt, Shawn Michaels would have skillfully handled the promotion. He was a *WrestleMania* veteran, a wonderful and charismatic athlete who understood all aspects of the business, especially the importance of marketing and promotion. It would have been difficult, though, to ask Shawn Michaels to help out with the promotion of *WrestleMania 13* when there was no chance he'd be participating. No one wanted him to show up merely as window dressing.

The responsibility for carrying the promotion of *WrestleMania* always falls on the participants in the main event—in this case, Sycho Sid and The Undertaker. Sid was at his best on the microphone, spitting out insults and challenges, frothing at the mouth, veins popping, eyes bulging. When he was on, he was great, and his performances brought a lot of attention to the event. But Sid wasn't always on; sometimes he wasn't even *there.* For example, Sid failed to attend an important press conference in Chicago because he had somehow missed his flight. A decision was made to hold the press conference without him, but it was an uncomfortable situation for everyone, especially The Undertaker, who was suddenly put in a position of having not only to carry the press conference, but to do so in a manner that contradicted the nature of his character as well as his own personality. The business is simply not supposed to work that way. Each person has a job, a role, and in the promotion of *WrestleMania 13,* it was Sycho Sid's job to do the talking.

It was our good fortune that The Undertaker was a real pro (I guess you'd have to call him a *black*-collar worker). Throughout his career he had maintained a steady and professional effort that eventu-

OPPOSITE: Sid grimaces from The Undertaker's nerve hold.

ally led him to the top, and his behavior and attitude during the promotion of *WrestleMania 13* was a perfect example of that professionalism. I think a lot of people who follow sports-entertainment were happy to see The Undertaker rewarded for his hard work at *WrestleMania*. He took the championship from Sycho Sid with a big-time performance in the biggest match of his life. The sheer physicality of the main event—two men of that size hoisting each other above their heads—compensated for the lack of a great story line. When you see a six-foot-eight, three-hundred-pound man body slam another man of equal size . . . well, you have a hard time believing your eyes. The Undertaker won the match with his aptly named finishing move, the Tombstone Piledriver, in which he turned Sid completely upside down and slammed him to the canvas.

Maybe it was appropriate that the Prince of Darkness was the winner of *WrestleMania* number *thirteen*. This was, after all, one of the most unusual *Wrestle-Manias,* and one that at times seemed to have a dark cloud hovering over it. Certainly The Undertaker's victory was celebrated in a manner not typical of previous *WrestleMania* main events. As The Undertaker knelt in the ring, a long arm extended menacingly out over his fallen opponent. There was a noticeable lack of pyrotechnics and rock music; instead, the entire arena was awash in a blue-black light, with sounds more akin to a funeral dirge or a thunderstorm than a Fourth of July party. It was a significantly different feeling, and while the fans obviously enjoyed themselves, their reaction was not a roar of celebration; rather, it was as if they were thinking, *We've just cheered this guy to the championship. What have we done?!*

RIGHT: When the smoke clears, The Undertaker captures the belt.

OPPOSITE: Some 60,000 of Shawn Michaels's hometown supporters jammed the Alamodome.

The People's Rookie

You can trace the career arc of virtually every World Wrestling Federation superstar simply by looking at his *WrestleMania* appearances. It's a truism that the Federation can do no more than put performers in prime positions and give them an opportunity to succeed or fail. Talent, charisma, and diligence will eventually win out. The fans respond to these things, especially at *WrestleMania*. In the case of Bret Hart, Shawn Michaels, and Stone Cold Steve Austin, it's interesting to see the way they start out at one position, as undercard performers, and then rise to superstar status over the course of a few years. The same is true of the character we now know as The Rock.

In 1997, The Rock was known as Rocky Maivia—a clean-cut, physically impressive wrestler with an unparalleled pedigree. Rocky's father, Rocky Johnson, was one of the sport's first African-American superstars; his grandfather, Peter Maivia, was a Samoan High Chief and a legendary wrestler in his own right some two decades earlier. Rocky had grown up in the business, and that certainly helped facilitate his meteoric rise through the ranks. At this point he was just two years removed from his football days at the University of Miami and less than one year removed from wrestling's minor leagues. Already, though, he was the Intercontinental champion.

Rocky's character was not close to fully developed, which at least partially explains why his match against the Sultan ended with an assist from Rocky Johnson. The Rock, as everyone knows, is something of a misanthrope. He almost always stands alone. He needs help from no one. But after this match, when Rocky Maivia was ambushed by multiple competitors, including the Sultan and the Iron Sheik, Rocky's dad was quick to come to his aid. As his shirt was ripped from his back, it was obvious that Rocky Johnson was

OPPOSITE: The Rock—then called Rocky Maivia—and father Rocky Johnson.

BELOW: Rocky greets the mysterious Sultan with a dropkick.

still in great shape. And in an odd but captivating mirror effect, Rocky John-son and Rocky Maivia began throwing those familiar large right hands—big, overhand punches that wiped out the entire ring. In the end, as 18,000 fans at the Rosemont Horizon cheered, father and son stood alone in the ring, embracing. Knowing The Rock's understanding of family and history, it's safe to assume that this was a pretty special moment for him and his father. In any sort of high-level athletic endeavor, it's rare for a father and son to have an opportunity to share the stage. Rocky Maivia's character would undergo huge changes in the coming year, but the memory of his first *WrestleMania* would linger.

OPPOSITE: Rocky levels his adversary with a high cross body block.

BELOW: Father and son celebrate the Inter-continental title win.

Stone Cold Says So

WrestleMania 13 will be remembered as the event that signaled a new direction for the World Wrestling Federation, in the person and perfor-mance of Stone Cold Steve Austin. In the past, Stone Cold's character would have been consid-ered a heel and fans would have detested him. He was a scowling, brooding, foulmouthed, beer-drink-ing loner. Dressed in black and bowing to no one, Steve Austin was the ultimate wrestling rebel, and fans responded with unprecedented adulation. In the weeks and months leading up to *WrestleMania 13,* as the Texas Rattlesnake repeatedly attacked the reputa-tion of his opponent, the beloved Bret Hart, a strange thing happened: the fans made the antihero a hero.

With Ken Shamrock acting as referee, the match between Stone Cold Steve Austin and Bret Hart turned into one of those hard-core events that take on a life of their own and become legendary. At one point, Bret tossed Stone Cold into a set of metal steps, opening up a large gash on Steve's head. The rules governing the match dictated that the first person to submit would lose. Despite bleeding profusely, Steve Austin fought on.

After the match—which ended with Stone Cold passing out and Bret Hart being declared the winner—the middle portion of the ring was soaked with blood. And while this was clearly a show, with a predetermined outcome, there was no way to pretend that the blood wasn't real. The World Wrestling Federation strives to protect its performers, and is not necessarily fond of delivering a match that produces excessive gore. Sometimes, though, it does happen, just as gruesome injuries occur on the football field and basketball court, and in the boxing ring. But this match was an indication of where *WrestleMania* was headed: to a level of intensity previously unseen in sports-entertainment. And without a doubt, it established Stone Cold Steve Austin as the company's biggest, toughest star.

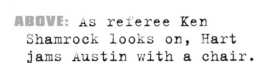

ABOVE: As referee Ken Shamrock looks on, Hart jams Austin with a chair.

RIGHT: A bloodied Stone Cold Steve Austin refuses to quit.

OPPOSITE: The Rattlesnake takes the edge over Bret Hart.

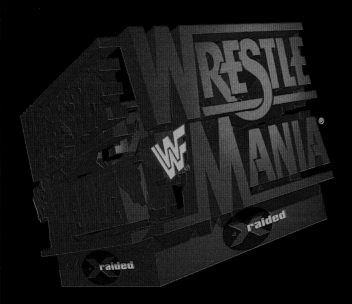

World Wrestling Federation Championship Match:
Shawn Michaels (Champion)
vs. Stone Cold Steve Austin
(with Mike Tyson as the "special enforcer")

Special Challenge Match:
The Undertaker vs. Kane (with Paul Bearer)

European Title Match:
HHH (Champion—with Chyna)vs. Owen Hart

World Wrestling Federation Intercontinental Title Match:
The Rock (Champion)vs. Ken Shamrock

Dumpster Rules Tag Team Title Match:
New Age Outlaws (Champions)
vs. Cactus Jack & Chainsaw Charlie

Mixed Tag Team Match:
Marvelous Marc Mero & Sable
vs. The Artist Formerly Known as Goldust & Luna

Light Heavyweight Title Match:
Taka Michinoku (Champion)vs. Aguila

Plus, for the first time in the World Wrestling Federation:
Fifteen-Team Battle Royal

The roots of the World Wrestling Federation were firmly planted in the Northeast, so the city of Boston had long been considered as a site for *WrestleMania*. Quite frankly, though, the old Boston Garden, which had played host to many great wrestling events over the past fifty years, had lost much of its charm. It had become a dank, musty old building with uncomfortable seats and bad sight lines, in serious need of renovation. As such, it never really provided an appropriate backdrop for *WrestleMania*. But with the advent of the Fleet Center, a gorgeous new arena, it seemed the perfect time to place *WrestleMania* in Boston, where the World Wrestling Federation had long had a significant fan base. Coincidentally, and rather poignantly, I thought, *WrestleMania XIV* was held in Boston, the same week as demolition of the old Boston Garden was begun. So, literally across the street, as *WrestleMania* came to town and set up shop in the gleaming new Fleet Center, the legendary Garden was being torn down brick by brick.

By the spring of 1998, the World Wrestling Federation had embarked on a steady course to an edgier brand of sports-entertainment, and this was clearly reflected in the lineup at *WrestleMania XIV*. Shawn Michaels had regained the title, and while he was a popular champion, he was nevertheless something of a "bad-boy" champion—a little bit wild, arrogant, cocky. Shawn pushed

OPPOSITE: Austin shows Tyson the World Wrestling Federation's new "Attitude."

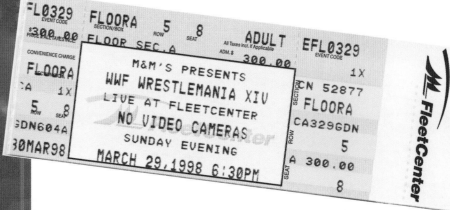

14

Fleet Center
Boston, Massachusetts
March 29, 1998
Attendance: 19,028

the envelope of what was traditionally considered acceptable behavior for a babyface. The same was true for several other characters on the card. Stone Cold Steve Austin, who would be Shawn's opponent in the main event, was by now the most popular and dynamic performer in sports-entertainment. His character's confrontation with Federation owner Vince McMahon was just beginning, and fans were reveling in his fondness for flipping the bird or cracking open a beer—or even "opening a can of one hundred percent whoop-ass!"—whenever the mood struck him.

And then there were the brothers grim—The Undertaker and Kane, two of the more unique and edgy characters on the company roster. The Undertaker, of course, was a top-tier star, a thickly tattooed giant who not only beat his opponents but purportedly robbed their souls in the process. Kane, as the story line went, was The Undertaker's long-lost younger brother, forced to wear a mask to hide the scars that remained after he was burned in a horrific fire during childhood. These two, spurred on by The Undertaker's manager, the cleverly named Paul Bearer, agreed to settle their family feud at *WrestleMania XIV*. Also on the card were Owen Hart, The Rock, Ken Shamrock, Triple H, and Mick Foley (in the guise of Cactus Jack), making this what has to be considered one of the strongest events in *WrestleMania* history.

ABOVE: Sibling rivalry: The Undertaker and half brother Kane.

OPPOSITE: Kane launches himself on his macabre brother.

Iron Mike With so many distinct and strong personalities involved, and with the overall program taking on what has come to be known as the World Wrestling Federation "attitude," it was perhaps inevitable that someone would suggest extending an invitation to Mike Tyson. Iron Mike had known more than his share of troubles in recent years. He'd spent three years in prison on a rape conviction; he'd been suspended by the Nevada State Athletic Commission after biting off a chunk of Evander Holyfield's ear during a championship match. Now he was marginalized, forced to sit on the sidelines as the sport of boxing sputtered along without him.

No one was really sure where Tyson's career was headed, whether or not he would be reinstated by the Nevada Commission, or even if he wanted to box again. Once regarded as

the most intimidating man in professional sports and potentially the greatest boxer ever, Tyson was now just a troubled guy in need of a payday and an outlet for his energy and creativity. So Vince reached out to Mike, not necessarily through his business advisors—Tyson's management team in those days seemed to change on a monthly basis—but rather through his friends and associates. A lot of hard work and persistence went into making the deal happen. And, significantly, one of the people most heavily involved was Vince's son, Shane McMahon,

Tyson, flanked by Austin and announcer Jim Ross, explains his role.

for whom the deal served as a kind of rite of passage. Shane, who has since proved himself an adept businessman (and performer), was chiefly responsible for handling the day-to-day dealings with Tyson and his advisors. Mike was arguably the biggest star ever recruited to participate in *WrestleMania,* and it was hoped that he would take a highly active role. There were several points when the deal could have fallen apart, but as negotiations went on, Vince became more adamant about getting Tyson on board. *WrestleMania XIV* was going to be a huge success with or without Mike Tyson, but from a creative standpoint, given the direction company had taken, the addition of Iron Mike, the self-proclaimed Baddest Man on the Planet, was deliciously synergistic.

Whether it made sense from a financial standpoint was another matter altogether. To the uninitiated, it might seem that having Mike Tyson on the marquee would guarantee the largest box office in *WrestleMania* history. But that wasn't quite true. We would sell 19,028 tickets to *WrestleMania XIV,* not nearly enough to offset the fee we'd be paying Iron Mike (rumored to be in excess of five million dollars), as well as the burgeoning cost of promoting the event. Even the Pay-Per-View take was unlikely to balance the ledger. As the negotiations went back and forth, I vividly remember a conference call during which the numbers were crunched, and it became apparent that there was virtually no way to earn back all the money it would cost to make this promotion a reality. Looking at it from a strict cost-management point of view, I made an impassioned plea to Vince.

"Look at it this way," I said. "Without Tyson, we will still do four or five hundred thousand Pay-Per-View buys, and make money. With Mike, we're probably going to lose money at seven hundred thousand buys."

Vince didn't even hesitate to respond, and his words laid to rest all of the doubts and finalized the decision.

"Don't you understand?" he said. "I'd rather lose money on eight hundred thousand Pay-Per-View buys than make money on four hundred thousand Pay-Per-View buys. That's how we grow the business."

As usual, Vince was thinking big . . . looking ahead. And so, after that declaration, there was no doubt about what we were going to do. One way or another, Mike Tyson was going to be a part of *WrestleMania XIV*. Interestingly, if you chart the growth of the World Wrestling Federation from March 1998 to today, you'll see a remarkable climb. In a span of two years, the television ratings have tripled, the company has gone public, and merchandise sales have gone through the roof. So . . . was it a smart decision to pay Mike Tyson however many millions of dollars to appear in *WrestleMania XIV*? It sure seems so.

Bad Boys and Girls

The World Wrestling Federation as a whole, and Shane McMahon in particular, worked closely with Tyson's advisors to convince them that Mike would not be exploited or humiliated. We viewed his participation as a good fit, something that would benefit both of us. On Mike's end, though, there was concern that his participation in *WrestleMania XIV* might jeopardize his chance to be reinstated by the Nevada Boxing Commission. After the Holyfield incident, the Commission had made it clear that it would disapprove of Tyson stepping into a ring—anywhere—until his suspension had expired. Vince McMahon assured Mike that if there was even the slightest possibility that he would be risking his boxing career, he could walk away from the deal. So we reached out to the Nevada Boxing Commission and explained Mike's role at *WrestleMania XIV:* he would be an "enforcer" and referee, but not a "combatant." Obviously, this was not an athletic event—in the traditional sense, anyway—but we were taking no chances.

Once the deal with Tyson was made, the entire theme of *WrestleMania XIV* came together. The concept, in a nutshell, was this: *a fall from grace*. Mike Tyson had been a prodigy, a teenager blessed with such

Mike Tyson grew up watching the World Wrestling Federation.

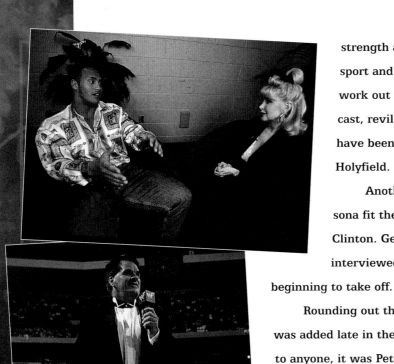

strength and talent that many boxing observers felt he would redefine the sport and one day be regarded as the greatest of all time. Obviously, it didn't work out that way, and at the time of *WrestleMania XIV,* Mike was an outcast, reviled and ridiculed for engaging in a barbarous act during what should have been a great boxing match: his heavyweight title fight with Evander Holyfield.

Another celebrity who took part in *WrestleMania XIV,* and whose persona fit the concept, was Gennifer Flowers, alleged one-time mistress of Bill Clinton. Gennifer was given the role of reporter, and among the people she interviewed, in hilarious fashion, was The Rock, whose character was just beginning to take off.

Rounding out the celebrity guest list, appropriately enough, was Pete Rose, who was added late in the promotion as an announcer. If ever the term "fallen hero" applied to anyone, it was Pete Rose . . . *Charlie Hustle.* Pete, of course, was one of baseball's greatest players, but he had been banned from the game for life after he was accused of betting on baseball. In the winter of 1998, Pete was in the news again because he had made some sort of motivational speech to one of his son's teams, and Major League Baseball had gotten all upset about it. We had already recruited him as an announcer, so it was inevitable that someone from the mainstream media, while covering this controversy, would question Pete about his role at *WrestleMania,* and that's precisely what happened. When asked if he was going to be physically involved in any of the matches, Pete responded with his usual mix of bluster and humor: "Why not? If anything happens, they can just throw me out of the ring on my face. Nothing could happen to this face, anyway."

Pete's role was to have been similar to the role played by Billy Martin some years earlier: a feisty ring announcer who would get the crowd all riled up simply by being himself. But after reading this quote in the newspaper, we thought, *Hey, this is our kind of guy.* So we gave Pete a call.

"Maybe you should be a little more involved," we suggested.

"Sure," Pete said. "I'm up for it."

Pete flew into Connecticut the day before *WrestleMania XIV*. The next day, *WrestleMania* Sunday, I took a limo up to Boston with Pete and three or four of his

TOP: Scandalous liaisons: The Rock and Gennifer Flowers.

CENTER: Baseball legend Pete Rose taunts the people of Boston.

BOTTOM: Kane silences the former All-Star with the Tombstone Piledriver.

associates. During that ride I explained to Pete what would be expected. Vince had mentioned the idea of having Pete insult the crowd. Pete liked that idea, and he and his buddies began throwing out suggestions. That was fine. But as the ride went on, Pete and his cronies became more and more boisterous, making fun of the event and the wrestlers involved—not so much Pete, but his buddies, who were really egging him on. It was making me very uncomfortable, and not just because their comments might be disrespectful to the men who put their bodies on the line every day. When celebrities are involved in *WrestleMania,* there is never any pretense that it's a fight to the death or anything like that, or that it's legitimate competition. Still, there is always the potential for serious

Austin catches Michaels's leg before he can deliver a kick.

injury in the ring, and you don't want anyone to get the wrong idea about what's going to happen. So, as the jocularity in the car continued, I decided it would be a good time to pull out the standard waiver form that anyone who participates in a World Wrestling Federation event must sign—a waiver that says, basically, if anything goes wrong . . . you're on your own.

"What's this?" Pete asked.

"Just the waiver. Don't worry."

Pete read the entire form. When he was finished, he looked up slowly, his eyes suddenly serious. "What exactly is going to happen when I'm out there?"

I shrugged. "Jeez, I don't know, Pete. Just sign it and we'll figure everything out later."

That changed the atmosphere in the limo pretty quickly. For the duration of the trip, Pete's buddies were more subdued. In the end, Pete was absolutely great. He signed autographs for all the wrestlers—he even signed for Mike Tyson—and he was thoroughly professional about his role. His first responsibility was to introduce the match between Kane and The Undertaker. Pete stepped into the ring, grabbed the microphone, and immediately began insulting the fans of Boston, whose beloved Red Sox had lost the 1975 World Series to Rose and his Cincinnati Reds.

"Hello, Boston," Pete said. "It's nice to come back to this city of losers!"

And . . . "Bucky Dent says hello."

And, most insulting of all: "You know, I was going to leave a couple tickets for Bill Buckner, but he couldn't bend over to pick them up!"

Not surprisingly, by the time Pete finished, the boos were cascading from the rafters of the Fleet Center. Amid the chaos, Kane entered the ring, and as he stepped through the ropes, the lights went black and flames shot up from all four ring posts. Kane marched to the center of the ring and grabbed Pete Rose. As the boos turned to cheers, Kane hoisted Pete over his head, turned him upside down, and delivered a tremendous piledriver. To his immense credit, Pete handled the move like a veteran of sports-entertainment, although the look of horror on his face as Kane lifted him skyward . . . well, I'm not sure that was all acting. By taking matters into his own hands, Kane earned the support of the crowd on this night. Even though he was beaten by The Undertaker, he was the star of the match, and his deft handling of the encounter with Pete Rose had energized the fans and set the tone for a rousing main event.

Opening a Can of Whoop-Ass!

In his role as chairman of the World Wrestling Federation on TV, Mr. McMahon had been doing everything in his power to back the champion, Shawn Michaels, and prevent Stone Cold Steve Austin from capturing the title. The snarling Mr. McMahon hated Austin, hated the idea that this bad-boy, disrespectful, Texas Rattlesnake ass-kicker would ever become the Federation champion. According to the story line, McMahon's hatred ran so deep that he was willing to enlist the services of former heavyweight champion Mike Tyson in his war against Stone Cold Steve Austin.

Mike Tyson

As the promotion progressed, Tyson fell in with the Heartbreak Kid and his gang, D-Generation X, which also included Triple H and Chyna. At a publicity event at the Government Center in Boston just two weeks prior to *WrestleMania XIV*, about 15,000 people witnessed a shoving match between Stone Cold Steve Austin and Mike Tyson. That encounter whetted the public's appetite and established the parameters for the main event: the battle lines had been drawn, alliances formed. There was no doubt that heading into *WrestleMania*, Mr. McMahon, D-Generation X, and Mike Tyson were conspiring against Stone Cold Steve Austin. To anyone who had been following the career of Steve Austin, however, it was clear that he was steamrolling his way to the championship. Never before had a World Wrestling Federation superstar experienced such a meteoric rise in popularity, and it would take more than this band of D-Generates to stop him.

ABOVE: Iron Mike tries to keep order at a press conference.

BELOW: Tyson appeared to have aligned himself with Triple H (left) and Michaels.

If you watch the tape of *WrestleMania XIV*, you'll notice a shot of Shawn Michaels looking into the camera just before he enters the ring and saying, "This one's for you, Earl!" He stays in character as he speaks, so that it sounds cocky, but in truth it was a heartfelt message to longtime referee Earl Hebner, who had fallen ill the night before and was hospitalized. The public didn't know anything about it, so it might have seemed as though Shawn was teasing someone. But he was completely sincere. In the World Wrestling Federation, you just never know when real life is going to intersect with the story line. Complicating matters further was the fact that Mike Tyson was serving as the guest referee for the match, which turned out to be one of Stone Cold Steve Austin's typically brutal fights. Both men took a lot of abuse, and in the end Steve used his favorite move, the Stone Cold Stunner, to immobilize Shawn Michaels. As Stone Cold covered the Heartbreak Kid, Tyson scrambled into the ring to deliver the final count: *One . . . two . . . three!*

Afterward, as Stone Cold Steve Austin stood in the ring, holding his championship belt, Shawn Michaels prepared to launch a post-match assault. But Tyson quickly intervened, flooring Michaels with a powerful right hand. After raising the new champion's hand, Iron Mike revealed that he had been a fan of Stone Cold Steve Austin's all along; he was merely *pretending* to be a D-Generate.

BELOW: Tyson's task was playing "special enforcer" at ringside.

OPPOSITE: With Iron Mike's help, the Steve Austin era officially commenced.

Later that night Tyson attended a post-*WrestleMania* press conference (covered by what was, without question, the largest media contingent ever assembled for any *WrestleMania* press conference). Choosing his words carefully, Tyson said he had enjoyed the experience and that he hoped to return to boxing in the near future. He was gracious and humble.

Stone Cold Steve Austin, as the new champion, labored under no such expectations. Near the end of the press conference he turned to face his nemesis, Vince McMahon, and snarled, "It doesn't matter what the organization tries to do. Nobody tells Stone Cold what kind of champion he's going to be. I'm going to be the hell-raising champion I want to be . . . and that's the bottom line!"

And with that, the tumultuous reign of Stone Cold Steve Austin was under way.

World Wrestling Federation Championship Match:
Stone Cold Steve Austin (Champion) vs. The Rock

European Championship Match:
Shane McMahon vs. X-Pac

Women's Championship Match:
Sable vs. Tori

Four-Corners Elimination Match for the World Wrestling Federation Intercontinental Championship:
Road Dogg vs. Val Venis vs. Ken Shamrock vs. Goldust

Triple H vs. Kane

Brawl for All:
Bart Gunn vs. Butterbean

Hell in a Cell Match:
The Undertaker vs. Big Boss Man

World Wrestling Federation Tag Team Title Match:
Owen Hart & Jeff Jarrett (with Debra) vs. D'Lo Brown & Test (with Ivory)

World Wrestling Federation Triple Threat Match for the Hardcore Championship:
B.A. Billy Gunn vs. Hardcore Holly vs. Al Snow

The Big Show Paul Wight vs. Mankind

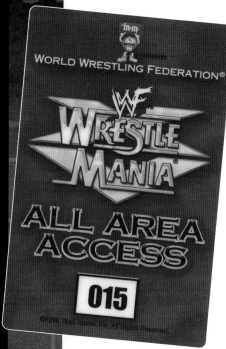

OPPOSITE: Evil "Mr. McMahon" knocks out the referee and takes his place in the main event.

For the third consecutive year, a brand-new, state-of-the-art facility played host to *WrestleMania*, a fact that speaks volumes about the growth and positioning of the World Wrestling Federation. Gone forever were the days when events routinely were held in 3,000-seat civic centers and armories; gone, too, were the days when it was considered appropriate to hold *WrestleMania* in just any arena. The crown jewel of sports-entertainment deserved a world-class home, and from now on it would have one.

Unveiled at the First Union Center, interestingly enough, was the World Wrestling Federation's new logo, which today is commonly referred to as the "attitudinal" or "scratch" logo. It's called the scratch logo because it literally looks like someone carved a WWF logo into a table. It evolved out of a meeting just prior to *WrestleMania XV* during which Vince McMahon explained that he felt the old block-letter chrome logo used by the company had become outdated, especially in light of the company's new attitude. The World Wrestling Federation was louder, flashier, and edgier than it ever had been, and the new logo needed to reflect that change.

"I have something in mind," Vince said to a roomful of people. "Think of a mug . . . frosted with ice. And think of using your fingernail to scratch the logo in kind of a rough style. That's what I want."

Before long, the scratch logo was born, and it's now become one of the most recognizable logos in the entertainment world. So there's no doubt that *WrestleMania XV,* in many ways, signaled the official beginning of the new age of the World Wrestling Federation, and the attitude that accompanied it.

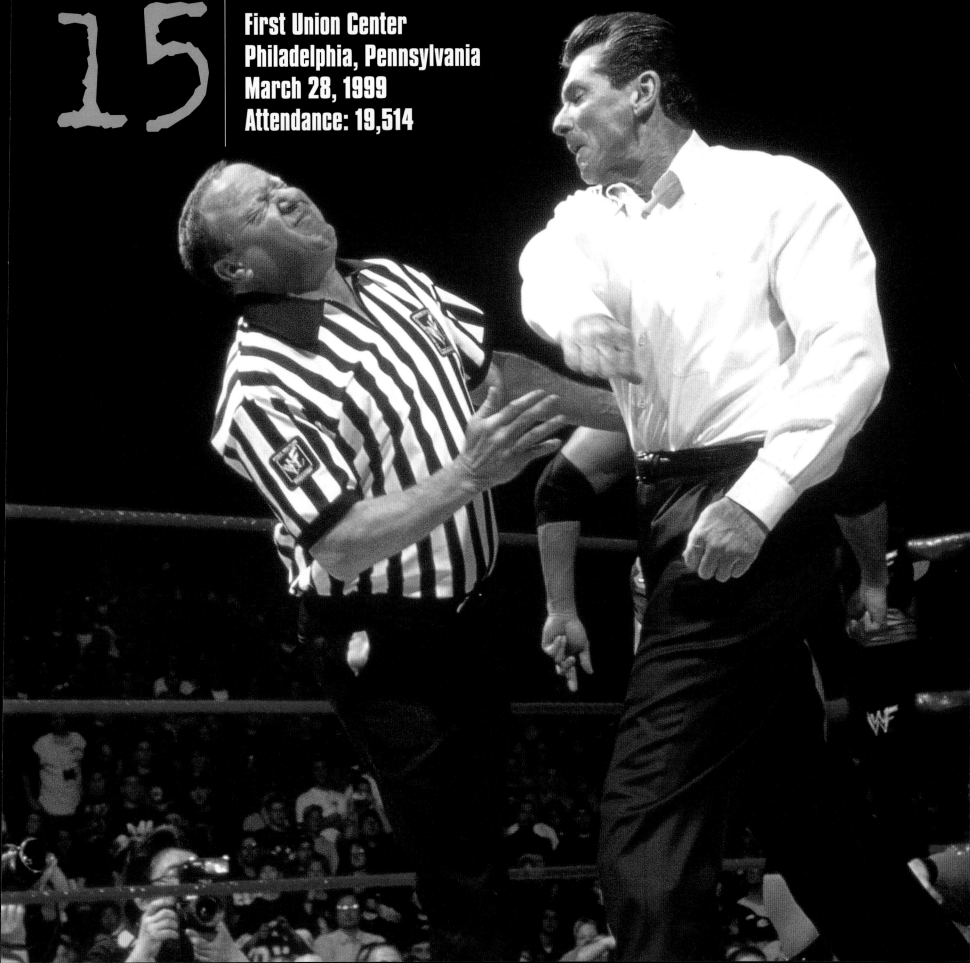

Stone Cold Steve
Austin's road to
success is paved
with his boss.

Mr. McMahon The adversarial relationship between Stone Cold Steve Austin and the smirking corporate demigod Mr. McMahon had erupted into a full-blown feud in the year following Austin's victory at *WrestleMania XIV*. In fact, on several occasions, it had escalated into physical confrontation. This signaled a significant change for both the World Wrestling Federation and its leader, Vince McMahon. Just three or four years earlier, Vince's on-air role had been limited to breathless, over-the-top broadcasting. His ownership and promotional wizardry had been very much in the background. While many knowledgeable fans understood that Vince was the genius behind the business, just as many fans—especially television viewers—considered him to be nothing more than an announcer. But when Vince McMahon, the de facto owner of the World Wrestling Federation, became *Mr. McMahon*, the chairman of the World Wrestling Federation . . . well, this set a new standard for brazenly blending fact and fiction.

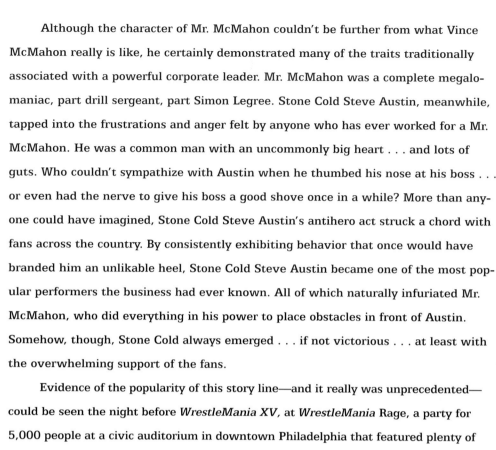

Although the character of Mr. McMahon couldn't be further from what Vince McMahon really is like, he certainly demonstrated many of the traits traditionally associated with a powerful corporate leader. Mr. McMahon was a complete megalomaniac, part drill sergeant, part Simon Legree. Stone Cold Steve Austin, meanwhile, tapped into the frustrations and anger felt by anyone who has ever worked for a Mr. McMahon. He was a common man with an uncommonly big heart . . . and lots of guts. Who couldn't sympathize with Austin when he thumbed his nose at his boss . . . or even had the nerve to give his boss a good shove once in a while? More than anyone could have imagined, Stone Cold Steve Austin's antihero act struck a chord with fans across the country. By consistently exhibiting behavior that once would have branded him an unlikable heel, Stone Cold Steve Austin became one of the most popular performers the business had ever known. All of which naturally infuriated Mr. McMahon, who did everything in his power to place obstacles in front of Austin. Somehow, though, Stone Cold always emerged . . . if not victorious . . . at least with the overwhelming support of the fans.

Evidence of the popularity of this story line—and it really was unprecedented—could be seen the night before *WrestleMania XV,* at *WrestleMania* Rage, a party for 5,000 people at a civic auditorium in downtown Philadelphia that featured plenty of pulsating music, dancing, food, and fun. Near the end of the party, a number of Federation superstars were introduced. Each came out on stage and said a few words about the next day's event. As Stone Cold Steve Austin took the microphone and began firing up the crowd with predictions of victory, Vince McMahon stood silently on a balcony. The promo ended with Steve pointing up at Vince and screaming, "You can't stop me!" much to the delight of the crowd, which went absolutely wild. Whether it was Vince McMahon or the character of Mr. McMahon on the balcony was anyone's guess, because he offered no retort. But it was a scene, with reality and fantasy colliding, and the fans eating it up, that worked just beautifully.

Gorillas, Chickens, and Butterbeans

The first match of the night was known as the Brawl for All Challenge, and it featured the Federation's Bart Gunn against a rotund, bald-headed boxer named Butterbean, noted for being the king of the three-round professional match. Boxer Vinny Pazienza, a multiple-title holder, was the referee for the match; the three guest judges were Chuck Wepner, the famous "Bayonne Bleeder" who once fought Muhammad Ali for the heavyweight title (and wrestled against Andre the Giant), and whose life served as the inspiration for the movie *Rocky;* Kevin Rooney, Mike Tyson's former trainer and Pazienza's current trainer; and Gorilla Monsoon, beloved member of the World

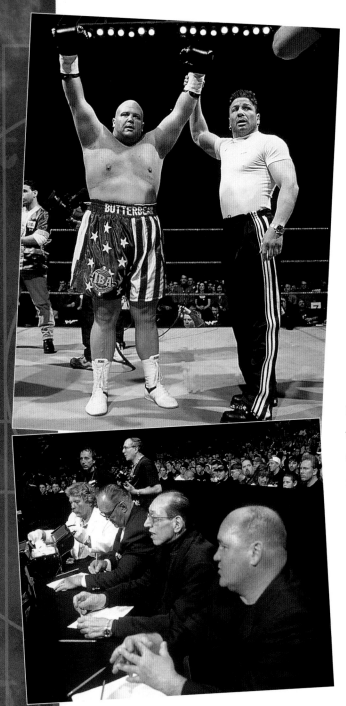

Wrestling Federation family, first as a wrestler and more recently as an announcer and executive.

By this time Gorilla was a shell of his former hulking self. Illness had begun to eat away at his body, and he was no longer an imposing figure. He was, however, still very much the gentleman, still quiet and soft-spoken, and I can recall vividly one of the most poignant moments of that evening, seeing Gorilla sitting by himself on a couch outside one of the dressing rooms, thinking and staring off into space. He sat there for the better part of an hour before the start of the event. People kept walking down the hall, saying hello, and while Gorilla was polite and always responded, it seemed as though his mind was elsewhere. As the event grew near, and the area around the dressing rooms became busier, the image of Gorilla, alone in his thoughts, yet surrounded by all of these young, vibrant athletes, took on a tone of sadness. It struck me that Gorilla knew he was about to hear his last cheers, that this would be his final appearance at *WrestleMania*. And indeed, it was. Gorilla would pass away just a few months later. When he stepped into the ring at the First Union Center, the crowd gave him a standing ovation—more, really . . . the loudest ovation of the night, and I realized that Gorilla probably knew exactly what was going to happen, and that when I had seen him earlier, he had been putting his whole career, and quite probably his life, in perspective.

One of the interesting things about this match was that the referee wasn't sure what to expect. Not until shortly before the Brawl for All actually began was Pazienza convinced that Butterbean and Bart Gunn were going to be involved in a legitimate fight; this was not a predetermined event, and I think that surprised Pazienza—he hadn't come to Philadelphia expecting to handle the responsibilities of a true referee. I believe he expected to be nothing more than a showpiece. I also believe that if you had polled the wrestlers in attendance, the vast majority would have predicted that Bart Gunn, who was considered an extremely tough man, would easily defeat Butterbean. After all, Butterbean, with three hundred soft, pasty pounds of flesh hanging on his frame, appeared to be an easy mark for someone like Bart.

Appearances, in this case, were deceiving. Butterbean, a devastating puncher, came out and hammered Bart twice in the first thirty seconds, knocking him to the canvas. Pazienza later said he would have stopped the fight right then had the knockdown not come so quickly. He wanted to give Bart another chance, so after making sure he was all right, Pazienza let the match resume. Not ten seconds later, Butterbean landed a ferocious punch that snapped Bart's head back and sent him flopping to the canvas. He was out cold before he hit the mat. It was almost scary to watch it, and in fact there was a moment or two in which Pazienza and the ringside judges were obviously concerned that Bart had been seriously hurt. It turned out that he was fine, but later Pazienza said, only half-jokingly, "Other than me, that's the hardest I've ever seen anyone get hit."

Butterbean's knockout of Bart Gunn was so quick and stunning, and so violent, that it put a hush over the crowd. Everything just sort of stopped. As Bart was recovering, seemingly out of nowhere, the Famous Chicken (formerly the San Diego Chicken) came scurrying into the ring and started taunting Pazienza. This appearance, of course, was part of the planned festivities, although no one could have known that a bit of comic relief would be needed at precisely the moment the Chicken was scheduled to run into the ring. The Famous Chicken bounced around a little, flapping his wings and clucking at Pazienza, until Pazienza finally gave him a little shot on the beak and knocked him out.

At that point the Chicken's performance appeared to be nothing more than a brief comic interlude, like a clown bursting into a rodeo ring. But two matches later, as Kane prepared to enter the ring for his battle with Triple H, the Famous Chicken came running up the ramp . . . and jumped on Kane's back! As the crowd howled in disbelief, the Chicken pounded on Kane, who spun around and flailed like a dog trying to shake off a fly. Eventually Kane slammed the Chicken into the ring apron and tore the Chicken's head off, revealing the man inside the costume: Pete Rose!

According to the story line, Pete had come back to exact his revenge on Kane, who had humiliated him a year earlier. But his plan had failed. Kane picked up the Chicken's head and threw it into the ring. Then he threw Pete Rose into the ring. Then Kane climbed through the ropes, hoisted Pete the Chicken over his head, and for a second consecutive year delivered a devastating pile driver, knocking Pete out. When interviewed an hour or so later, Pete Rose showed just how well he understood *WrestleMania* and the World Wrestling Federation by saying, "I thought I had him by surprise. It just didn't work out. I'll have something better next year."

TOP: Kane victimizes the Famous Chicken with the Tombstone Piledriver.

ABOVE: The Chicken is unmasked as Kane's old nemesis, Pete Rose.

An Electrifying Main Event

In order to become the Federation champion, Stone Cold Steve Austin had to take the belt from The Rock. Having been handpicked by Mr. McMahon to protect the company from the Texas Rattlesnake, the People's Champion was now known as the Corporate Champion. The Rock and Steve Austin were two of the hardest-working professionals in the business, and they had plotted out a match that would prove to be one of the most entertaining and athletic main events *WrestleMania* had ever seen. Adding to the tension and excitement was the participation of Mr. McMahon, who had worked hard behind the scenes to get Mankind installed as the referee of the Austin–Rock match. Earlier in the evening, however, Mankind—in the type of hard-core performance for which his alter ego, Mick Foley, has become famous—was so badly beaten by the five-hundred-pound Big Show that he had to be taken to a hospital. While Mankind was being carried out on a stretcher, Mr. McMahon entered the ring and began berating the Big Show, which obviously was a mistake. The Big Show, who stands seven feet tall, grabbed his boss by the neck and lifted him two feet off

TOP: Mankind rides Big Show's back, attempting to jam a sock-covered paw in his mouth.

LEFT: Mankind is carted off after another do-or-die, hard-core performance.

OPPOSITE TOP: The seven-foot Big Show gratifies the crowd by chokeslamming McMahon.

OPPOSITE BOTTOM: World Wrestling Federation President Shawn Michaels bars McMahon from calling the main event.

the ground. Just before passing out, Mr. McMahon was released. Instead of walking away, though, Mr. McMahon resumed his tirade, prompting the Big Show to respond with a huge, open-handed slap to the face that sent Mr. McMahon crumpling to the canvas.

After recovering, Mr. McMahon had the Big Show arrested. Police were called and the Big Show was led away in handcuffs. Now there was a problem. Who would referee the main event? Mankind was gone, and so was the Big Show, who by virtue of his victory over Mankind was supposed to have worked the title match. Well, the answer, naturally, was . . . Mr. McMahon. But as Mr. McMahon entered the ring dressed in black sweatpants and black sweatshirt, the theme music of Shawn Michaels began to play. The Heartbreak Kid, who had been sidelined with an injury, had become the acting president of the World Wrestling Federation, and therefore had veto power over the owner. With the fans cheering wildly, Shawn suggested that maybe Mr. McMahon hadn't read the rule book. If he had, he'd know that only one person can appoint a special referee, and that person is, of course, the president. Shawn ordered Vince McMahon from the ring and named Mike Chioda the referee for the main event.

Stone Cold Steve Austin against The Rock was, unquestionably, a match worthy of the hype that preceded it: two incredibly charismatic characters, each dressed simply in black trunks and black boots, with no enhancements of any kind to their physiques or personas. The Rock with very short hair, Stone Cold with no hair. It was just them and the ring and the crowd. Flashing back to the yellow and red of Hulk Hogan and the bright orange streamers of the Ultimate Warrior, it seemed as though the business had come full circle. The match of the year, the match the fans most wanted to see, featured two minimalist combatants. Yes, they were both great on the microphone; yes, they were gifted

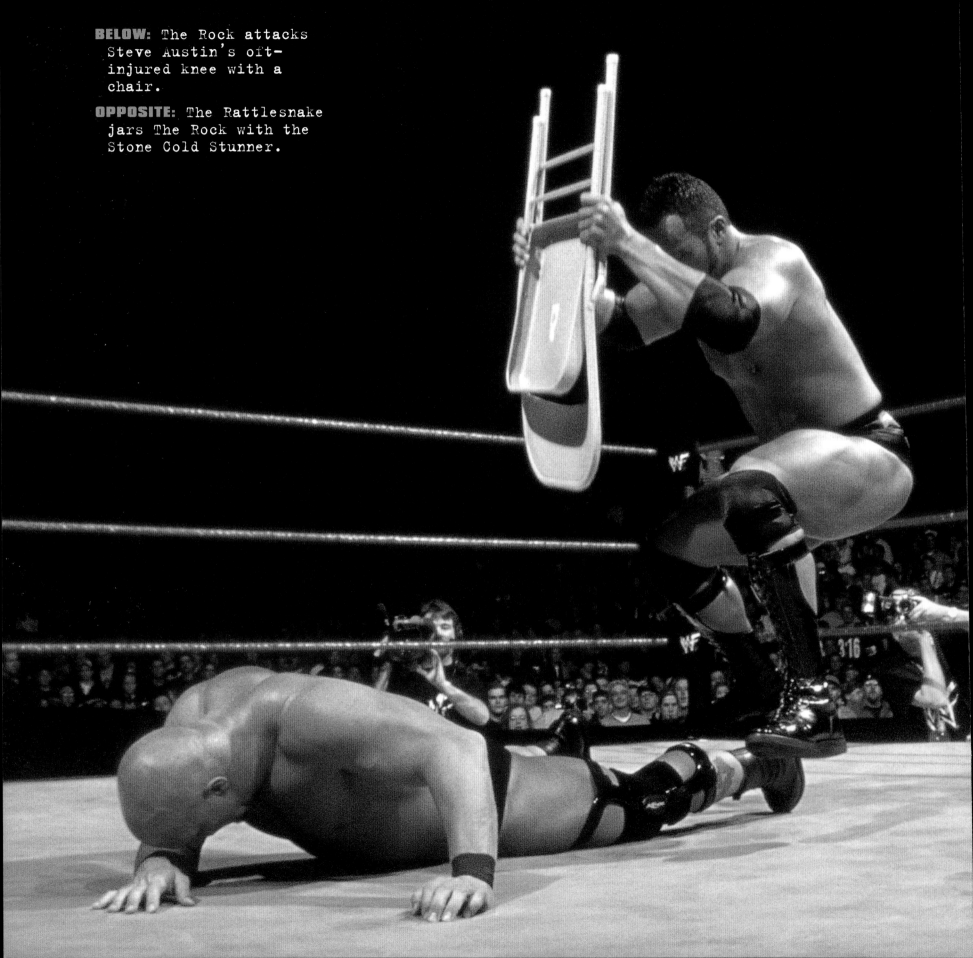

actors. But at this moment, they were merely wrestlers, and their black boots, black trunks, and chiseled physiques provided a starkness that the World Wrestling Federation and its fans hadn't seen in a very long time. It was markedly different from the sort of hyperbolic and theatrical events common at *WrestleMania,* almost like film noir.

Stone Cold Steve Austin was at the peak of his popularity around the time of *WrestleMania XV,* and The Rock was close behind. Together they put on a brilliantly physical match, culminating with Austin delivering a Stone Cold Stunner to win the title. The enduring image of *WrestleMania XV,* however, is not of Stone Cold Steve Austin pinning The Rock. The enduring image is of Stone Cold Steve Austin standing in the middle of the ring, one foot on the chest of a sobbing, beer-soaked (courtesy of a "Steve-weiser" opened in celebration after the match) Mr. McMahon, his face twisted in an exultant snarl, his hands clenched in fists, holding the championship belt high over his head.

Regardless of how long Steve Austin remains in this business, that will be the snapshot that typifies his brilliant career. It was a moment when everything came together perfectly—the athleticism, drama, and humor that combine to make *Wrestle-Mania* such a magnificent show.

OPPOSITE: The Rock can do little as Austin stands above his fallen form, talking trash.

RIGHT: Stone Cold Steve Austin succumbs to his opponent's treacherous Rock Bottom.

WF WRESTLEMANIA 2000

A WrestleMania First!
Fatal Four-Way Elimination
Title Match:

(Champion) Triple H
(with Stephanie McMahon-Helmsley)
vs. The Rock (with Vince McMahon)
vs. Big Show (with Shane McMahon)
vs. Cactus Jack (with Linda McMahon)

First Time Ever, Triple Threat
Rules for the Intercontinental
Title and the European Title:

Chris Jericho vs. Kurt Angle vs. Chris Benoit

Triangle Ladder Match
for the WWF Tag Team Title:

Hardy Boyz vs. Dudley Boyz vs. Edge and Christian

Kane (with Paul Bearer) and Rikishi
vs. X-Pac (with Tori) and Road Dogg

Six-Person Tag Bout:

Chyna and Too Cool
vs. Eddie Guerrero, Dean Malenko and Perry Saturn

Cat Fight Match:

Kat (with Mae Young)
vs. Terri (with Moolah) (with special referee Val Venis)

First Ever Thirteen-Man Battle
Royal for the Hardcore Title:

Crash Holly vs. Hardcore Holly vs. Tazz vs. Gangrel vs. Posse
vs. Headbangers vs. Viscera vs. Acolytes vs. Midian

Godfather and D'Lo Brown vs. Big Boss Man and Bull Buchanan

Al Snow and Steve Blackman vs. Test and Prince Albert (with Trish)

In the six months prior to the sixteenth edition of *WrestleMania,* the World Wrestling Federation had undergone profound changes. These changes were not restricted to image or attitude; rather, they encompassed virtually every aspect of the business— from economics, to popularity, to size . . . even to the name of the company itself.

In October 1999, the World Wrestling Federation went public. After operating as a family business in one form or another for nearly three generations, the Federation made the bold move of selling stock through an offering on the NASDAQ market. World Wrestling Federation Entertainment (WWFE), as the company is now known, became a public company. Although only fifteen percent of WWFE was made available, and the McMahon-held shares controlled ten-to-one voting rights, the IPO was a roaring success and placed the value of the company at more than one billion dollars. This move provided the capital and stability that at times had been lacking, and thus had prevented the World Wrestling Federation from accomplishing its highest goals. With the additional resources available, there really were no limits to what Vince McMahon and WWFE could reach . . . or at least strive to achieve.

OPPOSITE: The Rock sends Triple H to the mat with the Rock Bottom in the main event.

It was an amazing scene that greeted me the day after the IPO when I arrived at the McMahon residence to prepare for a meeting in New York. We assembled in the kitchen, Vince and Linda shared a quick cup of coffee, and we commiserated about our lack of sleep over the past few nights. Within minutes, however, we were en route to the city and deeply involved in planning the day's events. In their first day as *billionaires,* I could not detect any noticeable difference in either Vince's or Linda's attitude or demeanor. It was the same as always: "Okay, what are we gonna do today?"

Along with the financial fortunes of the company, the popularity and influence of the World Wrestling Federation had also risen to unprecedented heights. The new Thursday-night prime-time program *SmackDown!* had become the top-rated show on UPN, and was widely credited with saving the floundering network. And as if a prime-time network hit wasn't enough, *RAW,* the live two-hour program airing Monday night on the USA Network, had more than doubled its ratings in the past year and was the number one show on cable television. In fact, three of the top four cable programs were WWFE shows on USA.

This remarkable surge in popularity extended

The Rock and a fan enjoy each other's company at an auto-graph signing for *The Rock Says* . . .

far beyond the television screen. Live events were selling out at a rate typically associated with rock concerts featuring A-list performers. Sellouts became the norm, complimentary tickets were nearly impossible to find, and major events were selling out in minutes—usually months in advance. This frenzy also spilled over into Pay-Per-View buys, merchandise sales, sponsor sales, and publishing.

In fact, as a tribute to the size and breadth of the World Wrestling Federation influence, two books authored by Federation performers reached number one on the *New York Times* best-seller list. *Have a Nice Day* by Mick Foley and *The Rock Says* . . . by The Rock with Joe Layden both reached that lofty perch and remained on national best-seller lists for several months. This was a level of popularity that rivaled anything in *sports or entertainment*!

WrestleMania Without a Number

It was into this environment that *WrestleMania XVI* was introduced. In December, as usual, World Wrestling Federation patrons were invited to reserve tickets for the event. Our most important fans—those who attend the live events—were extended invitations while attending Federation events in the Los Angeles area during the first week of December. In a matter of days, well in advance of the mail-order deadline, more than enough orders were received to fill the Pond in Anaheim for *WrestleMania,* which was scheduled for April 2, 2000. Initially, it seemed like a good idea for the first *WrestleMania* of the new millennium to be tagged *WrestleMania 2000*. But by the time January had finally rolled around, everything had been "Y2K'd" to death. So, in typical WWFE fashion (whereby anything that becomes common is usually dismissed), the "2000" moniker was dropped, leaving this edition of the event with the same title as the original. The K.I.S.S. (Keep It Simple, Stupid) business model can work for the World Wrestling Federation as well as IBM.

WrestleMania Without a Main Event?

The company's current success did not come without challenges. The intensity of the crowds, the mushrooming television audiences, the sheer public demand—all spurred the Federation stars to new heights of performance. Collectively, this group of wrestlers attained a level of athleticism and entertainment previously unseen. Three of the biggest draws—Stone Cold Steve Austin, Mick Foley, and The Undertaker—faced serious injuries and physical challenges. Stone Cold underwent spinal surgery and was rumored to be retired. As *WrestleMania* drew near, it was apparent that neither he nor The Undertaker was ready to return to action.

Mick Foley, at the very moment that his best-selling life story had propelled him into the spotlight, had reached a point in his career when his body could no longer perform the tasks he required of it. Although speculation concerning Mick's future would run high, he would make one final appearance in the most unique *WrestleMania* match of all time.

Mick "Mankind" Foley became the first wrestler to crack the *New York Times* bestseller list.

While these superstars were sidelined, the responsibility of carrying the torch fell to The Rock and Triple H. The Rock, clearly "The People's Everything," was ready, willing, and able to ascend to the top, but according to protocol, that goal is achieved only after overcoming significant obstacles. The biggest obstacle in this case was known as Hunter Hearst Helmsley—HHH.

It's important to note that anyone involved with the World Wrestling Federation during this period would have had a hard time not recognizing the professionalism of the entire roster of wrestlers. But it's the active guys at the top who set the tone for the company and lead by example. These performers, and Triple H in particular, stepped up in a big way. Regardless of changes in the story lines, the sudden unavailability of opponents, or exhaustion brought on by an incredibly grueling schedule, they delivered top-notch entertainment to the fans. And that is always the ultimate goal of the World Wrestling Federation.

Earlier in the year, any fan might have been able to guess the *Wrestle Mania* main event: The Rock versus Stone Cold Steve Austin . . . or . . . The Rock versus The Undertaker . . . or . . . The Rock versus Triple H. But the story lines kept evolving, changing, so that in the weeks leading up to the show it was almost impossible to figure out what was going to happen. You could venture a guess as to where the main event story line was headed, but in all likelihood you'd be wrong. In fact, just sixteen days before the event, the announcement was made of a "Triple Threat Title Match" involving The Rock, The Big Show, and Triple H, with the championship belt at stake. Less than a week later, though, the main event would change and the drama would deepen.

Family Feud: *WrestleMania* Week

The evil chairman of the World Wrestling Federation, Mr. McMahon, by now had become a staple of the story line. Shane McMahon, playing Shane McMahon, Mr. McMahon's son, also had distinguished himself as someone to be watched. Shane had at first supported, then feuded with his dad. Linda McMahon, president and CEO of WWFE, and Vince's wife, had also occasionally been drawn into the ever-widening soap opera. Never before had the lines between reality and fiction been so blurred, and the weirdness was amplified by the fact that real-life people were playing themselves . . . sort of.

But without a doubt, the greatest surprise was Vince's daughter, Stephanie McMahon, in her role as . . . Stephanie McMahon, a provocatively dressed bad guy's girl who was ready to feud with everybody. Stephanie had initially fallen in love with a wrestler named Test, and had traveled to Las Vegas to celebrate

ABOVE: Stephanie McMahon's affairs of the heart had World Wrestling Federation fans buzzing.

OPPOSITE: Stephanie follows her "husband" Triple H to the ring for his Fatal Four-Way Elimination match.

Stephanie and Triple H show off their his and hers championship belts.

her upcoming nuptials. After imbibing too much, she fell prey to a spiked drink and ended up married to the wrong guy: *Triple H!* After her initial shock, and to the great dismay of her family, Stephanie began to enjoy her role as the wife of the Federation Champion. In fact, she reveled in it.

So, in the weeks leading up to *WrestleMania,* we had Stephanie happily flaunting her power and her marriage to the Champion; Mr. McMahon pulling every string he could to get The Rock positioned as Champion; and Shane McMahon backing The Big Show and angling for his man to capture the belt. I suppose it was inevitable that Linda McMahon, the one family member with a heart, would enter this circle and do something for the good of another. And that is what she did. Using her authority, Linda changed the main event of *WrestleMania* to a "Fatal Four-Way Title Match." The fourth spot would be occupied by the recently retired Mick Foley in his final appearance. So, finally, mere days before *WrestleMania,* the main event was made: The Big Show versus The Rock versus Mick Foley versus Triple H—with a McMahon in every corner!

Behind the Scenes During the buildup to *WrestleMania,* business for WWFE continued to boom. In fact, just four days before *Wrestle-Mania,* it was announced that NBC and WWFE would be partners in the XFL, a new professional football league. Not only would NBC own fifty percent of the league and televise its games in prime time, but the network also invested thirty million dollars in WWFE. This meant, of course, that General Electric, NBC's parent company—makers of everything from toasters to television shows to airplanes—was now in business with the World Wrestling Federation.

If not for Vince's long-standing friendship with Dick Ebersol, the clash of cultures of these two companies might have been too much to overcome. But Ebersol and NBC understood and respected Vince, and he returned that respect. At the press conference announcing the partnership, the stage was adorned with XFL and NBC logos, and the room was packed with reporters. When the questions concluded, Vince and Ebersol stood to embrace, and miraculously the XFL and NBC logos disappeared, and the backdrop switched in an instant to "*WrestleMania*—Live on Pay-Per-View!" The move prompted laughter and even some applause from the audience, but anger and dismay from one NBC media staffer. Most of the NBC executives were surprised but cool with it; however, this one particular staffer felt the gimmick had compromised and ruined the focus of the day—the XFL—and she was not happy. Well, all I can say is . . . welcome to our sandbox, where nothing is sacred.

Not even in the ring. Consider the case of Stephanie McMahon, who, when angered by Linda's inclusion of Mick Foley in *WrestleMania*, slapped her mother to the ground on *SmackDown!*. When Stephanie, a member of the WWFE advertising sales team, entered the staff meeting the following day, she was roundly booed. A week later, Shane attacked Vince on *RAW*, but there was no staff meeting that week. I posed the question to Vince: "Had there been a staff meeting this week, I wonder if Shane would have been booed or cheered?" Vince just smiled. Such questions, of course, are what the business is all about.

Back to the Pond In returning to the Pond in Anaheim, *WrestleMania* shared more than just a venue with *WrestleMania XII:* neither event placed any emphasis on celebrity guests. This despite the fact that many agents and celebrities in the L.A. area were contacting the World Wrestling Federation to discuss being a part of the event. I'm certain there were some pretty big names available, especially after Arnold Schwarzenegger had made a surprise appearance on *SmackDown!* a couple of months earlier. But to my knowledge, there were no serious discussions about anyone. Why? Well, when one of our marketers asked Vince about considering celebrity involvement in *WrestleMania,* he was told politely but directly, "Our guys are the celebrities now." And he was right. In fact, just two weeks before *WrestleMania,* The Rock hosted NBC's *Saturday Night Live* (Vince McMahon, Triple H, Mick Foley, and The Big Show also appeared), resulting in one of the show's highest ratings in years!

But perhaps the most glaring indication of the fame and popularity achieved by Federation superstars could be seen at the annual Fan Festival, which was now known as AXXESS. From a nice little party for invited guests of Trump Plaza at *WrestleMania IV,* the Fan Festival had evolved into a huge, interactive, multimedia event housed in a 10,000-square-foot space at the Anaheim Convention Center. AXXESS did exactly what the title suggested: it gave fans *access.* More than 30,000 people attended the two-day event. All four sessions were completely sold out. For the price of a twenty-five-dollar ticket, fans were treated to the sort of top-shelf event staged by the NCAA during Final Four Weekend, or the NBA during All-Star Weekend. You could

The AXXESS Fan Festival drew 30,000 "Fed-Heads" over two days.

visit the World Wrestling Federation television broadcasting truck, the auto racing team, a hall of fame booth; you could play any number of interactive games. Best of all, you could sit down with Howard Finkel, watch a broadcast of a famous match, record your own commentary, and leave with a commemorative videotape.

Despite all of this, a great number of fans spent a huge portion of their time at AXXESS waiting for autographs from superstars such as The Rock, Mick Foley, Triple H, Stone Cold Steve Austin, and The Undertaker. That fans were willing to stand in line, on average, more than an hour for an autograph speaks volumes about the level of popularity attained by the current roster of performers.

Christian vaults onto two rivals in the Triangle Ladder Match.

New Heights   The Pond was packed to the brim thirty minutes before the start of *WrestleMania*. Even before the first wrestler entered the arena, the energy level was as high as anything I'd ever experienced at a World Wrestling Federation event. The fans were chanting and cheering wildly, and it seemed as though every other person was holding some sort of sign. There was no way this intensity could be sustained over the length of a four-hour event, but clearly the crowd was ready to go. And they would not be disappointed.

There were two events that will be remembered from this *Wrestle-Mania*. The first was a Triangle Ladder Match pitting three different tag teams—the Hardy Boyz, Edge and Christian, and the Dudley Boyz—against each other in a spectacularly athletic and potentially dangerous match. There were three ladders and six very large men. The object, of course, was to scale one of the ladders and take possession of the tag team championship belts, which were suspended above the ring.

I had always felt that the Razor Ramon–Shawn Michaels ladder match at *WrestleMania X* was the most breathtaking and perilous match I'd ever witnessed. But not any longer. These guys were flying off the top of the ladder and out of the ring—falling sixteen, eighteen feet through the air. And while it's true that the wrestler on the ground breaks your fall a bit, just imagine how it feels to be lying there, waiting for a two-hundred-fifty-pound man to fall on your chest from that height. Whether you're expecting it or not, the impact can't be pleasant.

The Triangle Ladder Match was a vivid example of just how high the bar has been raised in the World Wrestling Federation. Every guy in this match was extremely athletic, and it seemed to me that at least a couple of them had to have had formal gymnastics training at some

point in their lives. I don't know how you can jump off the top of a twelve-foot ladder and do a full forward flip in the air—knowing that you're not going to land in water!—without having had some gymnastics instruction. It was truly amazing.

Toward the end of the match, two ladders were set up in the ring, with an eight-foot folding table spanning the gap between them, one end resting on the top rung of each. Multiple wrestlers climbed one of the ladders and crept out

Matt and Jeff Hardy's daring acrobatics may have qualified the Triangle Ladder clash as the match of the year.

onto the makeshift platform, only to be thrown off or yanked down. The intensity continued to build, with the match taking on the characteristics of an action-adventure movie—with no comic relief whatsoever. As the match reached one crescendo after another, I found myself muttering under my breath, "Someone please just go up there and get the damn belts. Let's be done with this already, before someone gets hurt." In the end, the team of Edge and Christian grabbed the belt and won the match.

But the outcome is not what I'll remember. What I will remember most is something I had never seen. In addition to the *oohs* and *aahs* you'd expect during a match such as this, there was also, on at least a half-dozen occasions, spontaneous applause. That was new to me. Wild cheering . . . boos . . . name-calling—all of these are part of a World Wrestling Federation event. Applause is not. I just think that in this case the crowd had no idea how to react. The athleticism and performances were so impressive and so unique that a certain level of respect seemed warranted. It was the type of response you might see when a pitcher leaves a game in the ninth inning after his no-hitter has been broken up: appreciative applause. And the fans weren't the only ones captivated by this match. Almost all of the other wrestlers were watching. You could see them peeking out from behind the curtain, or huddled around a television monitor in the dressing room. There was a general feeling that this was something you had to see, because you might not see it again for a very long time.

ABOVE: The Big Show gorilla presses the "People's Champion."

Fatal Four-Way That this *WrestleMania* appeared certain to break all Pay-Per-View records was a testament to the effort of the entire company, but especially to the unique nature of the main event. The Rock and Mick Foley, of course, were two of the biggest and most popular stars the business had ever seen; The Big Show, in the spirit of Andre the Giant, had also become immensely popular; and Triple H had developed into one of the best heels in the history of sports-entertainment. So you had these four distinct personalities, along with the McMahons, who were playing themselves, to a degree, which made for a main event that not only was unusual, but whose outcome was virtually impossible to predict. The air of uncertainty surrounding the Fatal Four-Way made this something that the fans really wanted to see. There was a moment on Saturday, the day before *WrestleMania,* when a number of WWFE employees were chatting about what was going to happen the next day. We were not part of the innermost circle, so for us, the outcome remained a mystery. We all had our opinions about what might transpire in the ring, and the strange thing was that every opinion seemed to make sense; you really could make a good case for any one of the four participants emerging victorious. If we felt that way, then it stood to reason that most of our fans were similarly intrigued.

The Rock delivers the Rock Bottom to the snarling leviathan.

One thing was obvious: this was not a main event that was going to end quickly, not with eight of the biggest personalities in the company all taking part. The various story lines had to be played out, and the participants had to be eliminated one at a time. The Big Show took the lead, spreading out the other three guys and using his sheer size to beat them down. The Rock, Triple H, and Mick Foley all came back, however, and hit The Big Show in unison. The Rock then pinned The Big Show, much to the delight of the crowd, reducing the Fatal Four-Way to a threesome. Triple H immediately turned to Mick Foley and implored him to join forces against The Rock. But Mick, former tag team partner of The Rock, would have none of that. Not one to fuss about his choice of allies, Triple H then asked The Rock to team up against Mick. Once again, Triple H was rebuffed. Ultimately, and appropriately, The Rock and Mick Foley double-teamed Triple H. But when The Rock tried to hit Triple H with the ring bell, Triple H ducked, and the blow caught Mick instead.

This was the setup for Mick Foley's farewell—at least as an active wrestler. He and Triple H eventually went over the top rope and out of the ring, totally destroying the announcer's table at ringside. As was often the case in Mick's career, the fall appeared startlingly painful. At the very least, Mick seemed to have the wind knocked out of him; he looked stunned. Unfortunately for Mick, a professional

Mankind unveils a special gift: a two-by-four wrapped with barbed wire.

wrestling match is not like a football game. The official does not call time out to see if you're hurt, or to give you time to catch your breath. Instead, moments later, someone is body-slamming you into the canvas. And so it was with Mick Foley, whose exit from *WrestleMania* came courtesy of a pin by Triple H. As he walked out, Mick waved to the crowd, which cheered wildly. Still in the ring, about to be retired forever, were some of the weapons Mick had used over the years—Cactus Jack's two-by-four wrapped in barbed wire, and Mankind's deadly Mr. Socko, symbols of one of the greatest careers in sports-entertainment.

After Mick's departure, the match moved inexorably toward its climax. As The Rock and Triple H battled inside the ring, Vince McMahon and Shane McMahon battled *outside* the ring. At one point Shane even hit his father with a television monitor, in the process apparently opening up a nasty gash on Mr. McMahon's forehead. Eventually, Vince wound up in the ring, with a chair in hand and a golden opportunity to make good on his promise to help The Rock recapture the title. As the crowd held its breath, Mr. McMahon drew back the chair

and prepared to club his "son-in-law." But at the last second, Vince took a step to his left and shifted his focus to a different target: The Rock! The crowd gasped in disbelief as The Rock crumpled to the canvas and was covered by Triple H. In a stunning double cross, Mr. McMahon had once again determined who would be the champion. The triumphant patriarch then stood arm in arm with his daughter, Stephanie, as the fans booed madly and hurled garbage into the ring. Never before had the title remained in the possession of a heel at *WrestleMania*. Tradition dictated that one of two things occur: the title had to change hands, or a good guy had to win. Apparently, the rules had changed.

But the People's Champion had his moment. The Rock eventually returned to the ring and ruined the McMahon family celebration by cleaning house with both Shane and Vince. Then, in perhaps the highlight of the entire show, he dropped the Rock Bottom and the People's Elbow on Stephanie McMahon. To say this was impressive and enlightening would be an understatement. While Stephanie is not a tiny woman, neither is she a bodybuilder. She is roughly half the size of The Rock, and she's spent very little time in the ring. For her to take these bumps was courageous, and it made for a spectacular ending to the biggest *WrestleMania* of all. As I watched The Rock bounce off the ropes in preparation for the

Vince McMahon bashes The Rock with a chair, aiding "son-in-law" Triple H's cause.

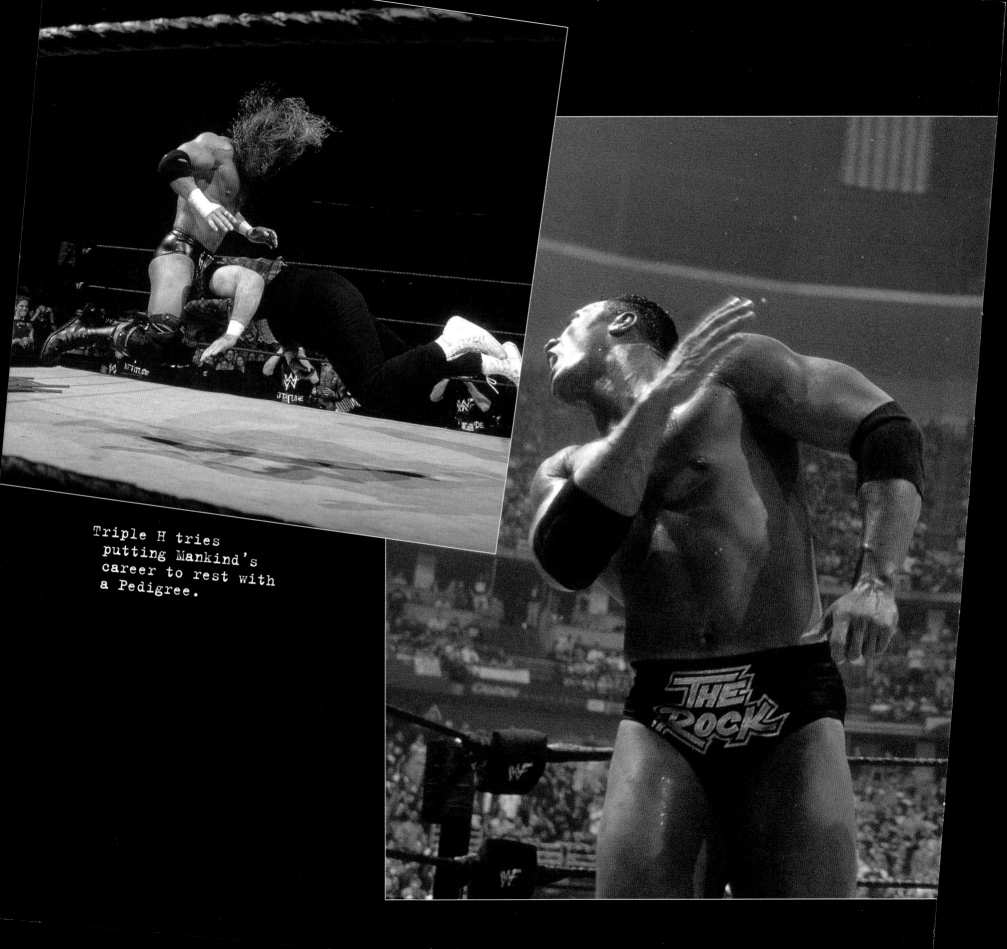

Triple H tries putting Mankind's career to rest with a Pedigree.

People's Elbow, and I listened to the roar of the crowd, I couldn't help but think of how much the business had changed . . . that in the year 2000 the most popular wrestler could body-slam an attractive young woman and still be a hero.

After *WrestleMania,* there was a reception for the WWFE family. Nothing fancy, just a nice dinner and an opportunity for everyone in the company, along with their relatives and friends, to relax and talk about the day. The reception started around ten or ten-thirty at night, and by eleven o'clock the ballroom was still relatively empty, which I found kind of surprising. So I ventured out across the hall and into a smaller room, which to my amazement was packed with wrestlers and their families, all of them entranced by a television monitor carrying a replay of *WrestleMania.* I'd seen this sort of thing from time to time—the performers will often watch a tape of an event while winding down and having a few beers. Usually the atmosphere is jocular, light, like the winning locker room after the Super Bowl.

This was quite different. These guys were mesmerized by what they were seeing. They were quiet, respectful, almost as if they were studying. They'd been at the arena for nearly twelve hours. The next night they'd be a hundred miles away, performing in another live, nationally televised event on *RAW.* They had earned the right to kick back, celebrate, do whatever they wanted to do for a few hours. But what they chose to do was to review their performance. That says a lot about their commitment to their craft, and the degree to which they invest themselves in their work. And that, of course, is the key ingredient to the success of *WrestleMania.*